MORE THAN ENOUGH

MORE THAN ENOUGH

Jasmine Herring

COPYRIGHT

Printed in the United States of America.
First Printing, 2017

ISBN-13: 978-0-9909919-6-0
ISBN10: 0990991962

the **B**utterfly Typeface

The Butterfly Typeface Publishing
PO BOX 56193
Little Rock Arkansas 72215

www.butterflytypeface.com
butterflytypeface.imw@gmail.com

DEDICATION

Jordan, Jayden, and Jarren it is your existence on this earth that gives me purpose in life. My love for each of you stems far greater than any words I could ever express.

Reach for the stars my Triple J and know that with God on your side, any dream that you have is in fact, possible.

I love you, mommy!

Everyone wants to know

how I got to where I am now

I asked myself that question too

And the answer is simple;

because of all that I went through

I wanted so much to be loved

The yearn for the affection

was much like an addicting drug

I found what I thought I needed,

but the person I wanted most

just couldn't see it

CONTENTS

LESLEY

CHAPTER ONE

LOVE ME, NOT

My husband and I had been married now for six months and with little guidance, day by day, I was trying to figure out how to be the perfect wife. Although I was not much of a cook, I always made certain that I marched into the kitchen after work and had a hot meal awaiting my husband's arrival, no matter how tired I was. I also made certain that my appearance was to his liking so that he would have a reason to want to come home each and every night.

It was habit too, prior to my husband's return from a busy day, to stand near the garage door as he entered, just to get a glimpse of his facial expression, as he placed his eyes on me, after being apart for many hours. My strategy was to reach for his hand and lure him inside with the scent of my cooking clouding the air.

On this particular day I could hear the garage door knob turn, but could not make my way to greet him fast enough as I was removing homemade rolls from the oven. I shouted out instead, "I'm in the kitchen honey. How was your day?"

The smile on my face and tone in my voice was always a key indicator of how happy I was to have my husband home.

With no response in return, I assumed that he either had his ear piece in which often blocked his ability to hear me or I simply was not loud enough. Whatever the cause for the silence, I made my way into the living room to greet my husband once more.

Just as I walked into the living room removing the stain covered apron to display a sexy red lace top that slightly exposed my breast, I noticed my husband resting on the couch responding to the constant alerts on his phone. He was a busy man and his drive for success was such a turn on and one of the many reasons I decided to marry him.

Still, receiving no verbal nor physical contact from my husband despite standing in his presence, I sat next to him not to interrupt, but to give a proper welcome home, "Hey baby? How was your day?"

Awaiting a response or some form of eye contact, I began to rub on his shoulders as I could tell that he had a long day from the exhausted look on his face and what I thought were emails that he was still responding to from work.

Not ten seconds into a massage that many would find comforting did my husband plant both of his hands on each of mine and remove them from his body. Embarrassed to say, it was common for my husband to ignore me and appear distant and although it did not take much to make him angry, just once I wish he would avoid bringing his problems home from work and act as though he were as happy to see me as I was to see him.

Not one to give up, I attempted to make conversation and massage his shoulders once more, "What's wrong honey? Did something happen at work today?"

Taking my concern as some form of attack, he stood from the couch letting out a big sigh, threw his arms up in the air with his cellphone clutched in one hand screen facing in the opposite direction, and began to yell which caused the pictures on our living room wall to rattle, "Can I come home just one day without you being all over me? Is that too much to ask for? Can't a man just come home and relax; damn."

I paused for a moment to process the last couple of

minutes and attempt to make some sense of what actions of mine could have caused such disruption in our home. Then I scoped out my surroundings to see if there were anyone else who walked in the door alongside my husband that he may have meant to direct his frustration towards.

As fast as he silenced his tone and appeared to have somewhat cooled down, yet another alert from his phone prompted him to utter one final frustrating statement with his back facing me, "I just want a day without you wanting to talk about work or being so chipper all of the time. Sometimes I think you live in a fairytale. Not every day is perfect Lesley."

My husband had just made it evident that no matter how much I attempted to learn of his day and console what I sensed were frustrations brought home, I was always going to be used as the scapegoat for his buried problems. However, despite his behaviors towards me, I was determined to show him that I was by his side.

I too stood from the couch near my husband, crossed my arms behind his waist, turned him around so that I could look into his piercing eyes that were filled with such anger, and attempt to calm him down with my subtle voice, "Baby, sit down and talk to me." I then guided my husband towards the couch we once sat on together and motioned for him to sit next to me with my right hand pressed against the cushion. While he sat and slowly cooled off, I knelt down on our carpeted floor to untie and remove his work shoes one by one.

I began to caress each and every toe on both sides of his feet hoping this would release any worries he may have held within. Looking through the corner of my right eye, I could tell that my husband was winding down as he had now leaned back on the couch and closed his eyes while I gently stroked his feet. Not wanting to ruin the moment, I kissed the backs of his heels while slowly releasing his feet to the ground and excused myself into the kitchen to continue the catering process.

In the kitchen, I sampled each item on the menu to ensure that all dishes were fully cooked and full of flavor that I hoped my husband would enjoy. After preparing his dish which was dressed with meatloaf, homemade rolls, macaroni, and green beans, I grabbed a fork from the kitchen drawer and proudly walked a meal fit for a king over to my husband.

"Here Baby, why don't you relax and eat your dinner?"

By this time, he was stretched out on the couch with his eyes glued to the television, making this the perfect moment to present to him a home cooked meal made with love. I placed the plate in my husband's face and watched as the steam from the meatloaf trailed up each nostril, arousing both his sense of smell and taste.

As much as I thought that his natural reaction would be to grab a hold of the plate and consume the food, the response instead was a push to my side to indicate that I was in his way. He then reached around me for the remote control that lay face down on the floor as if to ignore my efforts both in the kitchen and as a loving wife trying to make for a relaxing evening.

Filled with a state of both confusion and emotion, I sat the plate near the front of the television, hoping he would eventually come to. Replaying in my mind how I thought this evening was going to go as my husband arrived home and we placed our eyes on one another, I instead found myself walking away from him with tears that I could not hide as they were accompanied by a mild whimper.

Defeat was a hard pill for me to swallow especially knowing that I always placed my best foot forward. My husband never seemed to appear any other way, but angry and it was frustrating feeling as though one minute he is happy with me and the next he acts as though I do not even exist.

As much as I wanted to turn around and confess to my husband that his actions were upsetting, this too had the potential to cause an argument forcing me to stand down and continue up the stairs. At times like this I learned to voice my worry in the blank pages of my diary that held every teardrop consumed over the last couple of months. A diary that remained tucked away in the one place he would not dare to search; our wedding album box that contained both digital and audio footage of our special day which remained at the bottom of our walk-in closet slowly collecting dust. He had not once viewed any of the package with me and even when asked, did not show an ounce of interest either which made storing my diary here a safe haven.

Evenings that ended this way concluded sleeping alone with only my pillow to hold tight and keep me company. That was unless he was in the mood for intercourse in the early morning hours which he did not mind waking me for. That seemed to be the only time he ever expressed an emotion other than anger.

We were supposed to be in the honeymoon phase of our nuptials which I heard many of our family members brag about within the first year of marriage, but as each day passed us by I felt as though we were in the premature stages of a divorce. I could not force my husband to appreciate me, but I at least wanted to know that somewhere deep inside he did actually love me.

CHAPTER TWO

POINT OF NO RETURN

I could feel the warm sensation of the bright light hit my face as the sun arose through my window shade, but could not begin to open my eyes as they were filled with dried up tears that flowed last night, cradling me to sleep. As I began to stretch, I extended my left arm out to reach towards the other side of the bed where my husband would usually position himself, in an effort to kiss him good morning. All I felt; however, was a cold satin sheet that remained vacant reminding me of how our evening ended.

After rubbing my eyelids to free them of any and all tear residue, I lifted myself from the bed and opened my eyes to the start of a brand new day. From the glaring light that remained on in the walk-in closet along with a t-shirt and flannel pajama bottoms that trailed from the bedroom door to the bathroom, I knew that at least my husband had been upstairs once this morning and may still be present in our home.

The commotion coming from the first floor proved that my husband was in fact home and most likely on his way out the door. In need of his assistance, I knew that I had to hurry and catch him before it was too late. As I prepared to walk down the stairs, I realized that I had no idea who may be present in our home as my husband would often invite the neighbor over for coffee. I thought it best to cover my see-through lingerie with a bath robe that lay on the clean clothes basket in our hallway.

Following the aroma of coffee beans, the soles of my feet trailed along each wooden surface of the floor and led me to the final step of the staircase. There in the kitchen, I could see my husband pouring fresh coffee into his cup.

Taking the advice from yesterday, I did not want to approach him in a chipper manner for this would frustrate him, causing yet another argument that I did not want to have this early in the morning. I also did not want him to transition from a state of what appeared to be contentment to unhappiness and so I decided to alter my normal conversation to better suit his needs and ease my stress.

I tiptoed in the direction of the kitchen and just past our living room in search of possible house guests before approaching my husband with the favor that needed to be addressed. Upon realizing that no one else was present, but the two of us, I took a deep breath and delivered a faint greeting unlike my usual. This was sure to keep my husband sane.

"Hello Trent."

After taking a sip from his cup, Trent turned in the direction of my voice, but did not respond to my greeting or utter a single word for that matter. The nonverbal cues he gave off weren't the most inviting either and before I knew it, Trent's dialogue set the tone for the remainder of our short-lived conversation.

"Why would I want to say hello when you look like that?" Leaving me speechless, Trent walked away in preparation to head out of the door and I now thought twice about asking for his help.

Just before heading out of the door, he returned to the kitchen where I stood puzzled. I initially thought he had returned to embrace me and apologize for his poor choice of words, but instead he pointed to the top of my head and asked, "Do you plan on combing your hair today because nothing about your appearance strikes me as beautiful or worth taking out in public?"

It was bad enough having to hide my inner feelings for the sake of Trent's many reactions which often resulted in an argument, but for him to look at me, his wife, and not have anything pleasant to say whatsoever was a hurtful pain that struck at my self-esteem. He seemed most concerned with my appearance behind closed doors instead of giving me any credit for how I looked the few times we had actually gone out in public as a married couple. Hell, I received more compliments from total strangers than my very own husband.

"Trent, I just got out of bed," I said with a tremble in my voice. "I wanted to see you before you left for work this morning and I also wanted to ask you a favor." I often shivered when asking him anything because he made it so hard to talk to him. Even when I did gather the courage to speak, the response I longed for was never the one I received.

Acting as though I had not express a need to speak with him, Trent proceeded out of the side door where he pressed the button to open the garage which faced the driveway. My effort to grab and maintain his attention failing miserably as he was two steps faster and disregarding me every step of the way, forcing me to follow him all the way to his car. With no other option, I had to raise my voice and shout to alert Trent that I really did need him.

"Trent, would you stop for a minute please?"

You better believe that I was angry because the conversation was going nowhere and the disrespect was at an all-time high. I could not believe that I was literally chasing my husband outside of the house when our conversation began inside the walls of our very own kitchen. Now, I was being forced to stand outside, yelling in a bathrobe with rollers in my hair for all of our neighbors to see and speculate.

Just as I caught up with Trent, I placed my hand on the wide opened car door. He slammed the door shut in my face so hard, I was fearful that he'd shattered the bones that held my hand together. Determined, I knocked on the driver side window causing Trent to face my direction. Finally I was making progress in gaining his attention, even if I had to yell to do so.

With his eyebrows high and eyeballs popping out of each socket, Trent indicated with his behavior that he was highly irritated at my perseverance. "What is it that you need oh loud Lesley?"

His response was entirely sarcastic and I still could not believe that I had ran after him as if he had forgotten his wallet or an important document for work that he would be lost without. Those were the only reasons I could think of that a woman should ever come out in her bathrobe and rollers, chasing her husband. Nevertheless, I exhaled after holding back the frustration built inside and offered my question.

"My car keeps vibrating when I drive it," I said hesitantly and uncertain of his response. "Would you be able to take it to a mechanic this week and have it looked at?"

With no hesitation or any thought for that matter, Trent placed the car in drive, rolled the window up, leaving only a small crack and responded with a message sure to leave any spouse speechless, "Your car is not my problem," he said hatefully. "You drive it so you fix it."

Leaving me no room to respond, Trent drove off allowing the dust from the pavement to blow in my face. I stood there alone in our driveway forced to question where the morning went wrong. I had no idea what had gotten into this man. I lingered outside longer than I should have trying to make sense of the nonsense. I'd spent so much time chasing Trent that I completely forgot the fact that I too had to get ready for work.

I walked back inside of the house and closed the garage door. As I mentally prepared myself for the day, I could not help but fear taking my car to a mechanic all by myself. I knew nothing about cars and at least with Trent going in my place, the likelihood of him being taken advantage of was slim since as a male, he was probably more familiar with the automobile world than myself. Trent could get to the issue at hand and spot an overprice better than I could. Since I was behind schedule now thanks to Trent and he was clearly no help, I would have to place my car repairs on hold and pray that whatever the issue with my car, it would at least last through the end of the week while I figured out a solution for having it serviced.

STACY

Arriving to work often meant putting up a facade. Because I habitually hid my pain from others, my coworkers looked at me and my marriage as perfect and I played the role. They had no idea that I was being both emotionally and verbally abused and that my marriage was far from the fairytale depicted by my smile. You see, my reputation allowed for no tears. Indeed, I was known for being the mediator for others around the office. My work surroundings often took the focus away from my marital problems, which I was grateful for since work was the only place that I could escape emotional torment. It is not that my coworkers did not inquire about my marriage or point out discrepancies such as the discoloration of my eyes when I would arrive to work after a fit of crying, but I was not one to disclose my personal life which is why many thought that seeing me smile meant that I was living the dream. Because of the facade I'd created, it was far too embarrassing to reveal trouble in my home and my marriage. The fact that many of my coworkers stated that *my* marriage gave *them* hope in *their* own marriages gave me even more reason not to reveal the truth. Instead, I allowed them to believe that mine was the ideal marriage.

Upon entering the building of my job and scanning my work ID with the security guard who stood at the check in site, I heard a familiar voice calling my name from a close distance.

"Lesley?" The voice trembled.

I turned around to follow the voice and saw my coworker Stacy. Her eyes were blood shot red and as usual, she was drowning in tears. Thanks to Stacy's marital condition, I often found myself appreciating my husband so much more - if you could believe that. It is often stated that when you think you have it rough, there is someone elsewhere who has it worse and Stacy was living proof.

Stacy had been with her husband since freshman year of high school. They became pregnant their senior year and for this reason, both families forced them to marry. Unfortunately, Stacy miscarried two months later. Her husband was the only man she ever loved and in her heart, there was nowhere else she'd rather be. Despite the fact that he had cheated on her three times and fathered children outside of their marriage, he claimed that he loved her causing Stacy to remain in such dysfunction. She stood by her husband's side and remained a devoted wife, fighting for her relationship even if that meant that she was losing herself along the way.

I was never one to judge or offer personal opinion on the actions someone should take in a relationship. Instead, I was that ear to listen and shoulder to cry on, which is why I believe that many chose to confide in me including Stacy. In my mind, I could not understand why such a beautiful woman inside and out would stay with a man who did not value her. It was baffling to me knowing that she was pursuing a marriage with a man whose only efforts seem to be inflicting pain and creating constant reminders of his infidelities.

Jasmine Herring's, *More Than Enough*

Nevertheless, I wrapped my arms around Stacy in an attempt to console her and block others view of her current state. Because of her many public displays of emotional turmoil around the office, she had been the topic of conversation in the building for some time at work and not for good reason. Her emotional rollercoasters were becoming harder to hide, but as her friend I was not going to allow anyone to poke fun today for this was the worst I'd ever seen her.

As we were standing in front of the entrance to our building and obviously on display for the world to see, I pulled Stacy aside to see if I could get any information out of her as to what was making her cry.

"Stacy, what's wrong?"

Asking that very question must have taken her to a dark place because she had accumulated even more tears than when I entered the building to the point that she could barely breathe. Not knowing what else to do, I coddled her in my arms like a mother to a cub and guided her into the restroom on the main floor. Here I gathered tissue from an unoccupied stall and allowed her time to compose herself in private.

While she attempted to catch her breath and straighten

her face, I continued rubbing my friend's back as she needed much consoling. When encountering Stacy in this condition, I often asked what was wrong in an effort to make conversation and to let her know that I was here for her, but it was no secret where Stacy's pain originated.

Her tears made me think of my very own and a part of me could relate to her emotional state. Although Trent had never cheated on me, I did not feel that he valued me as his wife due to his distance and lack of affection. I too was starting to feel as though I was giving everything to a man who could not see or appreciate what I provided. Revealing much of my pain to Stacy could ease her worry as she often felt that she was the only one in a rough relationship, but this also meant that I would have to disclose my own marital troubles and I just wasn't prepared to do that. My friend was in need and nothing else mattered as Stacy was the focus at the moment.

Stacy placed her hands on the porcelain sink to give herself strength to fight back the tears long enough to tell me what was running through her mind and tearing her heart apart. Just as she lifted her chin and allowed our eyes to focus in on one another, I could predict the first sentence to come out of her mouth.

"He cheated again," she said in anguish. "A woman called me late last night and told me that she had been sleeping with my husband for over a year and that her one-month old son was his." For a brief second, my heart stopped as I could temporarily feel her pain, but I spoke not for she was unfinished recounting this unwanted conversation with a total stranger over the phone.

"She said that the only reason she contacted me was because he had cut all forms of communication and made it impossible to track. The woman told me that she was going after my husband for child support and to relay the message since he wouldn't step up on his own. Lesley, to hear this woman mouth to me that she had a son with my husband, with no regard for me as his wife, was not only embarrassing, but hurt so bad. She obviously knew that he had a wife to reach out to me and what, I was supposed to take this information and throw a party. You would have thought that accepting the first three would show him how much I love him, but again Lesley? I feel like I'm going to snap."

Stacy turned to the bathroom mirror and began pulling her hair with both hands as if she were having a mild mental breakdown. Not knowing what to do or how to help, I stepped back and rested my head on the wall nearby while she continued talking, "I look in the mirror and I do not even recognize myself."

Turning back in my direction and no longer crying, Stacy made a deep dark confession - one in which I did not know how to receive or if I should pretend that I never heard, "I am going to kill the next woman that says she is pregnant by my husband. I swear I am."

Thinking of all of the times that Stacy had been in this predicament, I wanted to throw my hands in the air and ask if she was surprised, considering he had already been exposed with the first three children. She had stayed with him this long forcing no type of ultimatum or setting ground rules. What did she expect? These were thoughts that I prayed would not accidentally leak from my mouth and roll off of my tongue for she was in no position to be criticized. If this child was in fact Stacy's husband's, it would be the fourth child making its entrance into the world while he was married to Stacy and I know that had to hurt. Not to mention, they had been trying to conceive for over two years now with failed attempts. Due to the fact that the other women were able to get pregnant at the hands of her husband, Stacy blamed her body for not being able to conceive since the miscarriage and for this reason, easily forgave her cheating husband. In her mind, which I honestly felt

Jasmine Herring's, *More Than Enough*

that she was losing, if she could give him the one precious gift he longed for, a child, she believed that he would have never sought to go elsewhere.

We had been here so many times, me holding Stacy's hand while she cried on my shoulder about her husband. Looking into Stacy's eyes forced me to take a step back for this day was different. Out of all the times she had revealed to me that he had been unfaithful, never had she stated that she wanted to kill anyone and I would be lying if I said I was not concerned. Stacy was on the edge of a mountain ready to fall and because I did not want her to take any course of action based on my spoken opinion, I listened, offering few words. Our conversation ended with a hug and me promising to always be there for her.

Out of the years that I had known Stacy, not once had I been introduced to her husband. From all that I heard, nothing she ever told me about him struck me as reason enough to stay and endure so much pain. One way or another, Stacy was going to reach her breaking point if she hadn't already. I could only hope that moment would not affect her to the point of no return.

CHAPTER THREE

TO THE RESCUE

An unexpected yawn exuded from my body as I concluded my final email of the day, forcing me to release all of my weight on the backrest of my chair at work. I removed the clip from my hair, allowing each strand to flow freely as I took a brief rest. Just as my body transitioned to the point of complete relaxation, I was interrupted by an irritating sound of rubber wheels rolling along the tile floors near my desk with an ever so annoying squeak. I opened each eye lid and looked up to find that a janitor had appeared on my floor and I felt compelled to check the time.

Lifting from my seat, I reached for my phone which was tucked away in a filing cabinet nearby and realized that it was after six. By this time, Trent was probably home ready to eat while I remained across town, sitting at my desk finishing up the day's work. Speaking of my husband, I glanced over at my phone a second time and realized that I had not once received a phone call nor a text all day. Between work meetings and consoling Stacy, I had been so consumed myself that I had not once stopped and checked on my husband which is why it would be unfair to get upset with him for not doing the same.

Wanting to get home as fast as I could, I gathered my materials from off of my desk, loaded them into my cross-body briefcase and bid goodbyes to all who remained in the building, including the friendly janitor who offered to walk me outside. Long days at work were draining and I simply could not wait to get out of my heels and just relax in the comfort of my very own home. No matter how tired I was though, nothing ever hindered me from fixing my husband a home cooked meal.

I was uncertain of what I would cook for dinner this evening, but I knew that once I stepped foot in the store, something would spark my taste buds and I hoped that it was quick. With it being just Trent and I, I found no reason to embrace heavy grocery shopping which meant that I had to make frequent visits to the store to prepare our meals even after extended work days.

I pulled into the parking lot of the nearest grocery store, but before getting out of the car, I thought it best to check in with Trent and let him know that I had made a stop at the store.

"Yeah."

That certainly was not the way that I expected him to answer the phone especially having no communication all day, but instead of nagging at Trent, I learned not to read so much into what appeared to be attitudes he exhibited.

"Hi Baby. What sounds good for dinner tonight?"

I truly hoped that whatever he decided, it was something easy and did not call for me to complete a lot of prep work.

"Lesley, it's damn near seven in the evening and now you want to know if I'm hungry. By the time you get home and cook, I will have already starved to death."

I had to remove my face from my phone for fear of Trent busting my eardrum with his vulgar tone. I could tell that he was angry, but this was no excuse for him to yell into my ear. He had taken this conversation overboard and to think, I gave him the benefit of the doubt for not contacting me all day and here he was flipping out because I had not done the same.

I could not tell if Trent's moodiness stemmed from work or if it was because I had yet to arrive home which is why I decided to take the higher route because someone had to be the voice of reason and bring this conversation down a notch or two. "Honey, I had meetings left and right today which is why you did not hear from me. I'm sorry that I was not able to call and check on you. You tell me what you have a taste for and I will be glad to make it for you."

I hoped that he would feel the sincerity in my voice and accept my apology so that we could move forward. All I wanted to do was make my husband happy and come home to a night without any arguing. For some reason; however, I just knew that Trent would not let up despite my efforts.

"I did not say that I missed you or that I even cared that you did not call today. What I am saying is, if you were not going to be home to make dinner, you should have said something earlier instead of having me waiting on you. I could have grabbed something on my way home."

He was not going to forgive easy and it appeared that I was going to have to reiterate my apology, one I wasn't sure I meant any longer, yet again. "Trent I said that I was sorry. Baby I am too exhausted to argue with you. I just need to know what you want for dinner so that I can get in and out of the store quickly."

"You are always tired. You're at that damn job more than you are at home. Just keep your ass there then."

All of a sudden, the conversation got quiet and the next thing I knew what was once a dialogue was now a monologue as Trent had disconnected the call. I was left to wonder if he truly accepted my apology which I only extended for sake of peace, but deep inside I knew that he hadn't. That man was likely to send me to an early grave with his short fuse. The whole point of calling was to check in as I felt that a wife should after being gone all day. Now it was up to me to figure out what we were having for dinner and to be honest, I was satisfied going home, calling it a night, and preparing a large breakfast the following morning. It was Trent that I was concerned about and as always, he showed the least bit of care for me.

Too upset to call him back, I threw my phone at the bottom of my purse and proceeded inside of the store where my mood would only get worse. Already frustrated, I walked into the grocery store only to find that the shelves were not stocked and the selection was minimal. From an outsider looking in, you would have thought that the customers were preparing for a winter storm that would leave them stranded in the house for days or that the grocery store was going out of business with the lack of product and disorganization that was visible.

With no energy to travel to any other store, I revisited each aisle twice until it was determined that the only ingredients they had available that made any sense combined together were those to make tacos. I released a sigh that erupted from my chest and rolled my eyes at the thought of standing on my feet a second longer frying hamburger meat, but it appeared that I had no choice if I wanted to feed my grumpy husband who was impatiently waiting on me.

Anxiously wanting to leave out of this store and get off of my feet, I quickly gathered a taco kit, sour cream, shredded cheese, a roll of hamburger meat, and one of the two remaining heads of lettuce that lay on the shelf before heading to the check-out line. It was at this very moment that I reached my limit with this day as well as the entire store.

Out of twenty-seven lanes, they had three that were available throughout the entire store and not a single one was an express lane. This meant that I had to wait behind large transactions with only five items in my hand. I knew that I was not getting home anytime soon especially since the person in front of me had two full carts, one in which her young child was pushing. If I were Trent, I would probably be mad myself which is why I would tolerate his upcoming behaviors when walking through the door.

My day just couldn't get any worse and fearing that I would lose my composure in the checkout line and possibly wind up on the ten o'clock news, I grabbed the nearest magazine and waited in line behind six other shoppers.

After standing in line for thirty-six minutes and reading an entire guide on home improvements, I was finally headed out of the store and on my way home to make dinner. It was time to put the pedal to the metal and offer some serious makeup to my husband; or at least I thought that it was.

Distracted by Trent's behavior over the phone and wanting to get in and out of the store as fast as I could, I paid no attention to where I parked my car. I had to walk up and down the parking lot with my two grocery bags and painful heels, pressing the alarm button on my keychain until the familiar sound led me to my car. After spending five minutes playing Marco Polo, it appeared in front of me on the opposite side from where I began searching. I threw my two bags in the passenger side of the front seat, thankful that I did not have any breakables and walked over to the driver side where I paused for a moment and rested my head on the roof of the car to regroup. I could have stayed in a still position all night as tired as I was, but had I done so, the parking lot would have become my home and the car, my bed. Exhaustion had set in strong and I had to pull myself together if I did not want to fall asleep at the wheel.

Upon opening the car door and getting in, I placed the key in the ignition ready to go, but my car failed to start. Assuming that I was too forceful towards the ignition, I gave a second attempt at a slower rate, but this did not work either. I guess I had stated too soon that my day could not get any worse because the worst had just greeted me with a hello.

Leaving the key in the unimpressed ignition, I began laughing in a sinister tone until that laughter transitioned into a scream. While screaming, it crossed my mind to take my frustration out on my steering wheel, punching it profusely, but I had no energy left to carry out any hostile action. Instead, attempting to gather what was left of my sanity, I searched for the car manual in the glove box where I thought I might find answers to get my car going and myself on the destination home. Scrolling down the glossary, I realized that I was wasting time. Even having the manual open, I was no mechanic and had no idea what I was in search of to begin the journey of finding a solution.

Jasmine Herring's, *More Than Enough*

Placing the manual back in the glove box, I began to replay the conversation in the driveway that I had had with Trent in regards to my car. I was more than thrilled to give him credit for my car failure this evening. I had given him the heads up that something was wrong with my car and even gone a step further and asked that he take it in to the shop which he declined. Now, I was left alone in a parking lot that was becoming dimmer by the second all because my car had finally given up on me and this was unsettling.

I may have let Trent off the hook for hanging up on me and being disrespectful, but his luck had just run out and I was about to sign, seal, and deliver an ear full.

Hastily grabbing my phone, I dialed the house number with great speed. I dared him to hang up this time or even think to flip the script on me. My big girl panties were held high and I was ready for war.

As soon as the first ring sounded through the speaker of my phone, I prepared myself to cut Trent off before he could even release a full breath, but instead I was greeted with an I don't care attitude and what sounded like a mouth full of food cutting me off.

"If you are calling to tell me that you haven't left the store yet save it. I already went and got me something to eat."

This MUTHA. Holding back the response I wanted to give, I had to remember that I was a Christian woman and refused to allow him to increase my blood pressure and take me out of character which he could easily do. By his own admission he knew that I was at the store and with an emphasis on "me," had the nerve to go out and purchase dinner for himself. How about honey I know you had a long day, just come home and I will take care of dinner. I mean who does that? I needed to run the tape back because this was absurd.

I was so taken back that I began to stutter, "Le le let me make sure I heard you right Trent."

I made certain that my voice resonated all the way to my house so that he could hear me loud and clear, "You went and bought yourself, a party of one, dinner when I told you that I was going to the store. Am I right?"

How was he going to talk his way out of this? I just wanted him to hear how ridiculous and selfish he sounded whether that was his intent or not.

"Lesley, you thought that I was going to wait on you to

come back from the store? I was hungry so I grabbed some tacos from Taco Bell. Whatever you bought, you can eat."

Tacos? Without stating another word to Trent, I searched my car front to back, top to bottom in search of hidden cameras because I had to be starring on the show *Snapped*. Somewhere in this very parking lot, an unmarked van was being entertained by my demeanor and constant outburst just waiting for the epic finale. After listening to Trent's lack of consideration, I could do nothing, but place the phone in my center console and punch my left palm with my right fist. I didn't even care that my windows were not tinted or who was watching my reaction in the car. I was fed up with this entire day and felt sorry for the next person to cross my path.

At this very moment I did in fact need my husband's help, but pride would not allow me to reveal my desperation. Stating nothing about the car, I gave Trent a taste of his own medicine and with the push of a button with my middle finger, thinking that he could see me flipping him off, I simply hung up the phone, leaving him in the dark to wonder about my current feelings or lack thereof.

The more time that passed while stranded in the parking lot made me rethink calling Trent, but I was not going to give in for he would forever hold that against me and make smug comments such as, "I told you that you would always need me," and I just didn't want to give him the satisfaction.

The parking lot was looking more and more like my home for the evening as I had previously foreseen because I could not think of anyone else to contact that had any experience working on cars. Even if I googled on my phone and found an automobile shop, it was after seven which meant most or all shops were closed for the evening.

With my night going south at a high speed and my head resting on the steering wheel, there was only one thing left to do; pray. Being an optimistic person, I knew that each day was not meant to be perfect and could usually smile through the frustration as I knew God was up to something, but on this particular day, I was having a hard time understanding God's motive which is why I began to pray hard and long. I prayed that God would help me see the lesson in this day and get me home safe.

Literally after mouthing the word *amen* and opening my eyes from a focused prayer request, I was startled by what sounded like knuckles tapping at my driver side window seeking my attention. Unaware of why or who would have reason to approach me, I hesitantly turned to my left and cracked my window just enough to hear the person speak, but not enough for him to place his hands around my neck and abduct me.

I was in no mood for shenanigans and allowed this unknown male to feel my built-up frustration with the stern tone in my voice. If his intentions were not well, he was about to get a rude awakening because he was messing with the wrong one, "WHAT?"

The gentleman, dressed in a tailored navy-blue suit, backed away from my window and placed his hands in the air as if to signal that he meant no harm and understood my vibe, "I'm sorry to bother you miss, but I noticed that your head was not moving and I just wanted to check and make sure that everything was ok."

This was either God rapidly responding to my prayer, a man looking to hit on me, or a hit man sent to kill me. I had yet distinguished which he was, but it wasn't getting any earlier and I had no other options, but to feed in to possible seduction on his part alone if there was the slightest chance that he may be able to assist me.

All I could think in my head was God please don't let him take advantage of me when I say that my car won't start if I should even disclose that information. I'm married and in no interest to leave or cheat on my husband and I am too young to die. I really needed a sign here on what to do.

Squinting my eyes together and squeezing the steering wheel with both hands as I was about to expose the fact that I was stranded, I exhaled all of the air that was holding my fears inside and spoke, praying that these were not my final words, "My car won't start."

With no verbal response, the unknown man reached inside of his pocket causing my entire body to leap over into the passenger seat all while extending my left arm towards the button on my driver side door to roll my window up completely leaving no possible entry into my car.

The stern Lesley had just become the fearful one. Why hadn't I just placed my stubbornness to the side and called my husband? Now I was playing the game life or death and I knew at this very moment that I was going to die, but unaware of the weapon of choice he was reaching for. Praying that he would just leave, yet another knock sounded from the driver side window and I could do nothing, but expose my fears in the form of a high octave shout, "LEAVE ME ALONE."

Remaining near my car, the man spoke through the glass while giving off a weird chuckle which brought more insight to just how crazy he actually was, "Ma'am. Just look up for a moment."

My heart racing, I looked up slightly with one eye open and the other tucked under my right arm, still sitting in the passenger seat, to find a business card attached to my window which read Timothy McWilliams owner and operator of Tim's Auto Solution. This was too good to be true, but I was not yet convinced that he was in fact a mechanic due to his physique and business attire. I slowly climbed back into the driver seat where I examined the business card displayed through the glass. Maybe this was in fact God and here I was about to turn down the assistance of an angel he sent to respond to my prayer. I needed to shape up and fast before this man gave up and walked way.

Placing slight trust in the situation, I more comfortably rolled my window down and reached for the business card that Timothy extended to me. Rather humiliated learning that this man was the real deal and having behaved in such a manner that anyone would walk away and opt not to help any further, I was not sure what words to state now that my eyes had been made aware. I thought it best to open up and be somewhat honest, "I apologize for my behavior. I have had a long day and all I want to do is get home and go to bed."

Knelt down and elbow on the driver side door, Timothy smiled at me and asked, "Did you think that I was going to kill you?"

Smirking slightly knowing that in the back of my mind those were my sentiments exactly, I thought that a little white lie wouldn't hurt, "No not at all."

With a smirk on his face, Timothy responded, "Sure."

After brief conversation as I could tell that he just wanted me to feel comfortable being in his presence, Timothy excused himself and reached in through my window, attempting to start my car. Observing that it would not start as I already knew, he asked me to remove myself from the driver side seat as he held the door open for me. He then got in himself to release the lever that allowed him access to what was under the hood.

"Here, I want you to hold on to your keys and start it up on my signal."

Timothy got out of the car and escorted me back inside, his hand pressed against my lower back. Thinking that I was about to get a strip tease, he unbuttoned his blazer in front of me, folded it and lay it on the roof of my car. He then walked towards the front of my engine, unbuttoned the cuffs to his white button-down shirt, rolled the sleeves up, and lifted the hood. Here, I observed a perfect stranger coming to my aid and my own husband had not once called back since hanging up to see if I was ok with it being so late in the evening.

Timothy quickly took my mind away from Trent's lack of care and failed rescue attempts as he commanded for me to give the car another start, "Start her up for me."

I placed the key in the ignition and sure enough, my car started. This being the only relief that I had received all day, I felt extremely overjoyed. I jumped in the backseat like a grasshopper where my purse was stationed; removed my wallet from the inside and stepped out of the car with my checkbook in hand to demonstrate my appreciation.

"Thank you so much! What do I owe you?"

He walked over towards me while wiping off his hands with a towel he pulled out of his back pocket and placed his newly cleaned palm over mine which had already begun writing a check with the information seen on his business card.

"Knowing that your car starts is payment enough. From the look, you are in need of an oil change and your battery does not have a lot of life left in it which explains the car failing to start. Hold on to my card and call me tomorrow. I wouldn't want you to find yourself stranded again."

My checkbook remained open and I still wanted to give him something. I mean, not only had he gotten on his knees to talk to me in a suit and offer his assistance, but he also got his white button down dirty which either he did not notice or did not care.

"I certainly will give you a call, but please allow me to give you some type of compensation."

Without knowing, I had placed my palm onto Timothy's chest expressing my want to repay him and it wasn't until I felt his heartbeat that I quickly snatched my hand back and placed it against my side where it rightfully belonged. "I don't feel right driving off not giving you anything."

Timothy took from my hand, a pen I had begun writing his check with and circled a number on the business card asking one request, "If you really want to do something for me, just text me on this cellular number and let me know that you made it home safe."

I was not satisfied with his response, but I could understand a man not wanting to accept money from a female and respected his stance. As we prepared to part ways, I wanted to extend my appreciation one last time before departing. "Thank you again!"

After grabbing his blazer, he walked back towards the hood of the car where he let it down gently, turned back towards me, and said, "You're welcome beautiful."

As much as I tried to hide it, I released a smile as those words placed a tingle throughout my entire body. After the day that I had, it was nice to not only receive some assistance with my car after my husband left me destitute, but a compliment as well which was something I had not heard my husband give since being married.

While in route to my home, it was Timothy's candid behavior that forced me to rethink my introduction inside of the house as my mood had since changed. The original plan was to walk in filled with venom as Trent had gotten dinner without me and most importantly had not come to my rescue. Instead, I proceeded in with a smile remaining on my face. Although Trent had not been there for me when I needed him, God sent Timothy to my aid and I could not complain for my car was temporarily fixed and would soon have all of the repairs it needed thanks to a total stranger who happened to be the owner of a repair shop. Talk about an on-time prayer response.

The night was almost over and I just wanted to take a hot bath and fall fast asleep in my bed whether that meant Trent would join me or not.

I walked into the kitchen which is where I was accustomed to placing my car keys and emptied the grocery bags inside of the refrigerator as making dinner was no longer a factor. To no surprise at all, I found remnants of Taco Bell which he had left on the floor as well as the countertop for me to clean. Still, I remained grateful to be home and found no sense in sulking over the fact that my husband was a slob or that he had blamed me for the increase in the utility bill, but was the one to leave the lights on in not only the kitchen, but also the living room which he occupied neither.

Taking a deep breath before walking up the stairs to our bedroom, I trailed slowly step by step for I was not certain of what would transpire between the two of us. Upon arrival, I found our bedroom door closed which caused me to open it gently and once inside, I realized that I needed not think of anything to say because Trent was sound asleep, laid across our entire bed leaving me no space.

I stood over his body wondering why he had not waited up for me. He had not once checked on my whereabouts and had not bothered to wait up to make sure that his wife had arrived home free from harm and danger.

Nodding in disbelief and turning my head away from the man that I was becoming unfamiliar with, I undressed myself in preparation for bed no longer wanting to soak in a hot bath. Once clothed in my night wear, I softly tapped Trent as I wanted to lay my head down as well, but I received no movement. It seemed as though I would have to position myself on the couch this evening if I wanted a place to lay my head, but before I closed my eyes for the remainder of the evening, I completed an excerpt in my hidden away diary.

Tonight's excerpt would be a reflection of the day that I had. After finally being able to put the long day to rest and relax in the comfort of my home, I took a moment to revisit each part of my day and realized that it wasn't as traumatic as I made it seem. Sure Stacy came running to me about the same problem, my days at work left me drained, and the grocery store was far from organized in many ways, but these were minor moments in my life that made me think about how grateful I actually was.

Stacy came to me because she found that I was a great friend which is something we all need. Work was draining, but I liked my job and it paid the bills. Although the lines were long at the grocery store, God supplied me with the means to purchase the items I needed and most of all, I had stressed over car repairs and God sent me a person to be there just when I needed.

Thinking of car repairs, I was reminded of Timothy's only request; text him once I arrived home. This simple request made me contemplate honoring however. The entire time that I had been with my husband, I had never socialized with the opposite sex unless it pertained to work and felt strange about texting another man and assuring him that I was home safe. I toyed with the business card in my hand while looking back and forth at both Trent who was snoring in the bed and my cellphone. After going back and forth about whether or not it was acceptable to text Timothy, it dawned on me that in some way this was just a business transaction. The text pertained to my car and was completely innocent. Timothy had not once asked for compensation for his time or labor and walked away wanting nothing more than to make certain that the work he had provided lasted long enough to get me home.

The decision was made; I would send the text message and schedule an appointment for further repairs the following morning. That was neither inappropriate nor disrespectful to my husband especially when he told me that I needed to take the necessary steps on my own to get my car fixed. I stood from the floor where I completed my diary entry, yanked a pillow from underneath Trent's legs that lay on our king-sized bed, and went downstairs to send the text with confidence and no regrets.

Contemplating on what I would say so that there was no doubt about professionalism and also no guilt texting Timothy while Trent remained sleep upstairs in our home, I took a brief stroll around my coffee table in the living room before realizing that I was being silly. I was not a girl in high school and this was far from a childish crush. I was an adult and this was strictly business. All I had to state was that the car made it home. How hard could that be?

Without any more thought, I held the card in one hand and texted away with the other.

"Timothy, this is Lesley. Just wanted to inform you that the car made it home safe. Thank you again. Good night!"

The task that I made so very complicated was complete and after pressing the send button, my work was done and rest had begun.

CHAPTER FOUR

I CAN DO IT BY MYSELF

I awoke to the sound of the garage door slamming shut and anxiously arose from the couch as I did not hear my upstairs alarm go off. As fast as I could, I sprinted up the stairs into my bedroom to find that my alarm had been purposely turned off. Not only had Trent left without saying a word or questioning my whereabouts last night, but had also failed to tell me that my alarm had gone off causing me to be late for work.

Today would have to be a hair up no make-up kind of day as I had no extra time to heat up my flat iron nor apply foundation to my face. I showered as fast as I possibly could, realizing that Trent had used all of the hot water as well. The ice cold feeling in the shower made my time inside all the shorter. Once covered with a warm towel to alleviate the chill, I scurried along and searched my closet for an outfit that was both classy, yet comfy to go with the bun above my head. With minimal time to search, it was decided that I would wear a pair of dark denim jeans with a white camisole underneath a black blazer. I added a statement necklace to give my attire the pop that it needed, grabbed a pair of red heels from the bottom closet, and prepared myself for an amazing work day despite being late.

Retrieving my briefcase from my bedroom closet, car keys and cellphone downstairs, along with a banana from the kitchen as I would not have any time to stop for breakfast, I made my way towards the front door where I hoped that I would not forget anything.

Feeling a sense of *deja vu* sitting in the driver seat of my car, I sent a quick prayer up above remembering last night's fiasco, placed the key in the ignition crossing my fingers, and reversed out of the garage with no complications. I was all clear for the time being, but as Timothy had stated, it was time for a few repairs which I would contact him this afternoon to set up the necessary appointment.

I waited until I reached the first red light, a block from my home, before scavenging for his business card to make sure that I had it to set up the appointment this afternoon. With no luck, it dawned on me that I had left the card on the coffee table at home after texting him last night. The good thing about the text that I was oh so afraid to send was the fact that it stored his number in my phone so long as the message had not been erased.

Before I could even search for the message once approaching the red light, I was interrupted by Trent's phone call. This was a call that I was not anticipating on answering at the moment and chose not to. I was not going to allow him to spoil what I knew would be a great day. Whatever the need, it was not important enough as he could have spoken to me this morning after turning off my alarm and leaving without even a simple hello. My safety and car were more important than Trent's morning tangents and seeing as though we had not spoken this morning, I could only imagine the hell he wanted to start over the phone.

I waited for the call to end completely instead of pressing the ignore button which I thought to do. That would have been a completely different argument had I sent him straight to voicemail. Once the ringing stopped, my phone notified me that I not only had a missed call, but unread text message as well. It wasn't like Trent to reach out using both phone call and text which made me a little worrisome. My nerves had officially been set off and I could not help, but to think that something might actually be wrong and that this wasn't just another episode of Trent's.

Jasmine Herring's, *More Than Enough*

Unable to concentrate on the road any longer, I utilized my right signal in order to maneuver through traffic and pulled over to the nearest parking area which happened to be a gas station. I needed to have complete focus on my phone and upcoming conversation to make sure all things were well.

Bracing myself for whatever Trent needed to say, I opened the message and to my surprise, it was not a message from Trent at all, but one from Timothy responding to the message I sent last night which read, "Thank you for letting me know that you made it in safe. A beautiful woman such as yourself should never be stranded. Please do not hesitate ever to contact me if you run in to a future situation and need help again."

Drained from all that occurred last night, I did not think to stay up and wait on a reply message. He probably thought that I was ungrateful which the case wasn't at all. I had to contact Timothy and redeem myself. I was in fact a thankful citizen and had to let that be known before the offer to fix my car would no longer be valid.

Pulling the number from the text message log, I braced myself for I did not know what type of mood he would be in as he received no response to the message he had sent five minutes after mine which some would take offense.

"Good morning. This is Timothy McWilliams."

Unsure of what to say, I remained quiet while in deep thought, hoping that maybe he would recognize my number and speak first.

"Hello, is anyone there?"

I could not believe that my lips were frozen shut which would make this the second time that I found it hard to speak to this man. He had stated hello a total of three times with the final hello coming off as pretty irritated. I knew that if I did not speak fast, he would hang up and I may never gather the courage to call again.

With a baritone voice, he extended his greeting one final time, "HELLO. IS ANYONE THERE?"

All of a sudden I felt as though someone had pushed me in the back, forcing all of the words I had planned to state up from my diaphragm and out of my mouth, "I'm sorry. I must have had my phone on mute. Good morning Timothy. I'm not sure if you remember me from last night, but this is Lesley." Why was I always nervous around this man? I was a natural born communicator and here I was afraid to mumble the word hello.

"Forget you? Never. How are you this morning?"

Thank God he appeared to be in a good mood which meant that I still had a shot of getting my car fixed. "Who me?" I was taken by surprise as I was not used to being asked how I was doing for I was the one who generally reached out to others.

Sarcastically responding, "You are the only woman that I am talking to at the moment, aren't you?"

"Haha Mr. McWilliams. I am doing well. Thank you for asking. I was calling in regards to my car."

I heard a gasp for air on the other end of the phone and could not help, but wonder if he had just had a medical emergency.

"Oh no. Did it stop again?"

His sense of concern almost came across as if he were afraid for my life. I had to quickly ease his worry for I felt he would soon faint, "The car is just fine. You had mentioned last night that it was in need of an oil change and replacement battery so I was just wondering when I could set up an appointment?"

"Oh ok. How about this Saturday at noon? Will that work for you?"

Outside of work, I was pretty open with my time. Despite constantly asking, Trent was not one to take me out on many dates which allowed vacancies in my life. I was behind closed doors so often that had I not had a job which allowed me to reveal my face in public, no one would even know that I existed. Although I knew that the day and time would work, I still felt the need to pretend as though I potentially had plans and placed him on hold to look at my nonexistent schedule, "Give me a moment to check my planner." I did not want to appear boring nor willing and ready to jump to anyone's demands as I had done enough of that with my husband.

After a short intermission, I took the phone off of mute as if I were some sort of call center and responded to his appointment offer, "Umm it looks like," dragging out the final words like I was going down a long itinerary, "that works well for me."

"Perfect! The address is on my business card if you

haven't thrown it away yet."

I wasn't sure of why he would think that I would throw his card away. Maybe he was upset that I had not responded to his text after all? Nonetheless, I still had the card. In fact, had I walked into my house, I would know exactly where to find it.

Not reading too much into his comment, I responded in an effort to give him some assurance that I wasn't this cruel woman he had depicted in his mind, "No. I still have it. I will see you tomorrow."

"Have a good day Lesley."

"You as well Timothy."

Had it not been for the SUV behind me blowing their horn as someone was in need of the air dispenser that I was parked in front of, I would have forgotten that I had to get to work.

Knowing that someone would be calling and checking on my whereabouts as I often led many boardroom meetings, I still drove at a slow speed as I continued to smile from ear to ear about my upcoming car repairs. My entire drive to work was filled with laughter and giggles. I was getting my baby fixed which made me feel victorious. In your face Trent. I had made the necessary appointment to have my car serviced no thanks to my husband and I could not have felt more accomplished. So excited, I gave no thought to call Trent back and did not care what the repercussion was.

CHAPTER FIVE

DO I NEED YOU

"Are you going to give me some before you leave?"

How convenient of Trent to ask for sex just as I was leaving out of the house, in route to the appointment he was well informed of and was even invited to attend. Not to mention that I had spent the entire evening last night romancing him just for Trent to continue focusing on his cellphone and paying me absolutely no mind. It had taken me nearly two hours of caressing from head to toe before Trent finally rolled over onto his side, placing the back of his head to the front of my face. Even then I wrapped my leg around his and used my foot to gently stroke his inner thighs assuming this would be the one act to arouse him and stimulate his sense of touch enough to want to make love. I even went a step further and used my hands to massage his genitals and still this ignited no intimacy.

Literally having one foot out of the door and I was supposed to stop, turn around, and assume the one and only position he was most fond of. His unromantic way of requesting sex was enough to make me want to continue walking out of the door, slamming it shut in his face, but as always, I irritably obliged.

As much as I wanted to leave, I also wanted peace in my home and walking out of the house would not only leave Trent sexually frustrated, but full of anger that he would use against me once I returned from getting my car repaired. In the back of my mind I knew that the more I gave into his needs no matter how they were delivered, the better chance I felt that I had of making him love and care more.

Knowing my husband all too well, this was going to be a quick act in which I needed not undress nor partake in any fore play.

As I got in my stance on the couch awaiting my husband, I could hear him unzip and lower his pants to the ground. He then placed both palms on my buttocks and began verbalizing his instructions, "poke that ass up in the air."

As much as I feared this position due to the pain that it caused, my husband loved it and as always, I aimed to please him. I found peace within a nearby pillow that muffled my painful cries and allowed Trent to have his way with me for I knew that the pain would only last a little while longer and was one step closer to his affection.

"Trent back up a little. You're going too far." He had struck a spot that caused me to flinch and accidentally kick him in the knee which I could tell made him very upset.

"Stop being so stiff and it won't hurt."

Pushing my lower back with his palm, Trent went right back inside, performing the same act as if to ignore my silent cries. He clearly found no remorse and certainly did nothing to accommodate my obvious pain. As much discomfort that was caused during intercourse, the most hurtful part of all was what he did after the short length that it took him to reach his climax.

Instead of ever ejaculating inside of me or wearing a condom to eliminate possible pregnancy which he feared, Trent always found it necessary to release himself on my back or stomach depending on the final position.

He made me feel like I was a one-night stand or some mistress he was trying to hide from the world. Here I was his wife and I am not saying that I was ready to have a baby at this very moment, but if it happened it happened. We were married and most married couples planned to conceive some point in the relationship in order for their family to grow. Trent on the other hand did not want children which I knew nothing of until after we were married. Instead, he used the pull out method to avoid fatherhood which he swore by.

"Why are you still sitting that way?" The excruciating pain from intercourse often caused me to remain in the still position Trent left me in once finished and I always knew this would start a debate between the two of us initiated by he himself. "You didn't even do any work Lesley."

In my mind I'm wondering how any couple could enjoy sex that lasted under two minutes and what work could actually be done in such a short time frame, but wanting not to hurt his pride, I allowed my thoughts to remain locked away in my head where they would never be released.

"I did exactly what you asked Trent." Never mind the pain that he caused or the fact that he left me to clean myself up after releasing his sperm all over my body, but always managed to clean himself off in front of me. His only focus was what I could have or should have done as if sex with him was always magical.

"If you did what I asked I would have been more satisfied Lesley."

Each comment that was made after having sex made me less excited for the next intimate moment. He had spoken so negatively in the past about our sex life that it was often hard to give my all because when I did, he still found reason to complain forcing me to reevaluate myself in the bedroom when he too played a role.

Spending too much time listening to Trent's belittlement, I noticed that the clock which rested on our fireplace mantle showed that I had thirty minutes before my appointment with Timothy and as I had no idea where the shop was located, I would have to cut Trent's complaints short.

I both cleaned and freshened myself up before grabbing Timothy's business card from off of the coffee table as I would need his address plugged into my GPS.

Knowing the response, I considerately extended one final invitation to Trent before walking out of the door, "Are you sure you don't want to go with me to the shop?"

With no time to wait on a response and hearing no movement within the house, I walked out assuming that had he

Jasmine Herring's, *More Than Enough*

been interested in accompanying me he would have been right by my side. I even waited a few seconds before pulling out of the driveway, blew the horn once, and then took off.

If I was able to make the appointment on my own, surely, I could point out whether or not Timothy's quote was overpriced without my husband's guidance.

I found myself needing Trent less as the days went on and if his patterns continued, I may not need him at all.

CHAPTER SIX

RIGHT ON TIME

Worried that I would miss my appointment, Timothy's shop happened to only be ten minutes away and even with Trent's morning escapade, I still had a few minutes to spare.

As I did not see Timothy anywhere in sight once I opened the door to the facility, I decided to look around as I had never physically been inside of an automobile shop before. From the looks of things, it appeared that his business was doing very well. He had a ten-man crew from observation, eight of which were out in the shop working on cars and the other two ensuring that customer service was on point at the front. The lobby was filled with patrons who were indulging in both coffee and donuts as they waited on their vehicle repairs, all seemingly content.

After inspecting the facility more than impressed, I awaited in the service line to check in and also inform Timothy that I had arrived on time for my appointment as being punctual was one of my mottos.

"How may I help you ma'am?"

Hearing the word ma'am was like music to my ears. Both servicemen were so polite and I knew at this very moment that my car was in good hands. I always said that first impressions were vital to the growth of any business and the way these two employees represented the company, it was clear that the shop had a bright future ahead. I stepped up to the front counter following the serviceman's greeting to complete the check in process, feeling as though I could not have selected a better shop even though coincidentally, the owner actually found me.

"Good afternoon. My name is Lesley and I have a noon appointment with Timothy McWilliams."

Just as I stated Timothy's name, I noticed the gentleman look up and smile at me. He then extended his left arm out and pointed his index finger towards the lobby. Curious as to why he was both smiling and pointing, but not checking me in, I turned around to see what had captured his attention. Behind me stood Mr. McWilliams himself dressed in a burgundy button-down shirt, tan khaki pants, and sunglasses that he had yet to remove from his face.

With a brief chuckle and arms stretched out to signal that he was in fact in the building, Timothy spoke with a bright smile, "Timothy McWilliams at your service. So formal of you to use all, but my middle name Miss. Lesley."

Timothy was the only person that could approach me in a sarcastic manner and still force laughter out of my system. Sometimes I felt that he could read my mind and knew just when I was having a bad day, forcing him to step in like superman, eliminating all of the enemies and bringing me back to a state of peace.

Too embarrassed to display the same animation that Timothy did in a lobby filled with customers, my response instead was an elegant good afternoon, "Good afternoon Timothy. How are you?"

He looked me up and down, slowly bringing his focus back to my face while biting down on his bottom lip, "I am doing amazing now. Why don't you follow me to my office?"

There were still seats available in the lobby which I was happy to sit in as I waited on my car to be serviced, but Timothy insisted on joining him in his office which I followed with slight hesitation.

Just before heading through the double doors that took us down a brief hallway, Timothy removed the car keys from my palm and handed them to a nearby tech, "Jim, please see to it that Miss. Lesley's car is taken good care of immediately. I already plugged her information into the system."

My car was in preparation of being serviced and as Timothy already knew the mechanical issues, I did not see the point of heading back to his office.

"I don't mind sitting out in the lobby with the other customers. Really."

Before entering into his office door which had his name engraved on the window, Timothy looked at me with his hand turning the door knob and said, "You are my VIP customer and I would offer nothing less than excellent service."

As much as I appreciated Timothy's kind gestures, I needed to make it clear that I was married before he thought to proceed with any further act or conversation that may cross boundaries. Even though Trent and I were in a rough space in our relationship, I was not going to do anything to disrespect our vows nor destroy our marriage.

I allowed Timothy to close the door behind us and just

as I turned around to reveal that I was married, standing before me was Timothy prepared to take the lead on the topic of discussion, "I don't mean to pry, but do you mind if I ask you a personal question?"

He pulled a seat out for me to sit in and rested comfortably on the marble desk in front of me awaiting my response with an inquisitive look on his face.

I had no idea what this man was going to ask and almost chose to walk out of the office with great speed as my comfort level had diminished. Remaining silent, I looked up at this gutsy man who had not taken focus off of my face and allowed him the floor to ask the million-dollar personal question that would either make me faint or rise from the chair and proceed out of the door in search of a new mechanic.

Making no promise to answer the question that may potentially cross the boundaries I was afraid of, I at least heard him out as it was clear that something was on his mind.

Tapping my fingers on the arm rest of the chair, I asked, "What would you like to know?"

Courageous enough to express the need to ask a question, Timothy had now become silent as if his courage had quickly turned into fear. He took a few deep breaths while staring at me and after an extensive period of silence, finally began to speak.

"And again, if this is too delicate I apologize, but the other night when you were stranded at the grocery store and placed your hand on my chest, I noticed a ring on your finger which tells me that you are married."

Had this man lured me all the way back to his office to make a pass at me where no one could hear me scream? If he did not hurry up and spit out whatever it was that he had to say I was going to be using some defense tactics.

Timothy stood from the marble desk that he had planted his body on and at first I scooted my chair back thinking he was coming towards me, but instead, he turned in the opposite direction and walked back to the chair, which rested behind his desk, finally releasing his question, "Why didn't your husband come to your rescue when your car stopped? Why isn't he standing in your place seeing that your car is taken care of? I mean, if I was married I would not think twice about coming to my wife's aid and she certainly would not be the one fixing her own car."

As nervous as I was speaking in front of this man and as much as I hid my personal problems from the outside world, it was something about the delivery of Timothy's questions that exposed tears from my eyes and made me realize that I was alone in a marriage that lacked a partnership.

The tears hindered my ability to respond and forced Timothy to walk over to me and extend a box of tissue while knelt down, "Oh Lesley. I did not mean to make you cry. I'm sorry for overstepping."

No one had ever seen me like this because I never allowed my pain to consume me. At times where I wanted to cry, it was someone else's problems that took focus away from my very own. Now here I had Timothy, a total stranger focused not on himself, but displayed concern on my behalf and as I had no personal information on his life to channel my emotion, my hurt had nowhere else to turn, but out in the open.

I accepted the tissue that Timothy offered which reminded me of the many times that I had extended kleenex to Stacy when learning of her husband's indiscretions and for the first time, I found myself on the receiving end, needing someone which even Stacy wasn't familiar.

After composing myself fully, I wiped my face and responded to Timothy's question with a sense of freedom to hold nothing back.

"You know, my husband was not always like this. I mean, before I married him, he showered me with love and affection. He took great pride in being a wonderful boyfriend and did everything he could to show me that he was my prince charming and that I need not look any further. A few weeks after our wedding, I noticed a drastic change in the man who had once swept me off of my feet and it was like our fairytale came to an end. His love and affection transitioned to a state of comfort. I felt like he no longer cared to try anymore. It seems that now that we are married, the fight he once had to keep me happy he no longer cares to pursue."

Part of me felt as though I had said too much, but at the same time it felt so good to finally voice my pain to a person who knew nothing of my life being this supposed fairytale everyone festered upon which is why I continued to disclose much so long as Timothy allowed.

"For sake of not arguing I've learned to tolerate a lot, but this past month has been the worse I have ever seen him. For the life of me I cannot figure out what has happened to turn him into such a monster. I keep hoping that he will form back into the man that I fell in love with because I don't know how much more I can take. The night that you found me at the grocery store, he and I had just gotten into an argument because I had yet to return home with dinner and he felt as though I was spending too much time at work. He did not bother to check on me after our fight which ended hanging up on one another, but at the same time I did not inform him that I was stranded either. I had such a trying day which is why you found me slightly hostile that I was accepting the fact that I was probably going to spend the night in the parking lot."

Pausing for a moment as tears started to resurface, Timothy eased in and took the floor, "In what ways do you feel that your husband has changed for the worse?"

I was entirely surprised that after all I had said, not once had Timothy pointed the finger at me or asked if I had done anything to bring my marriage to a possible end. He displayed a concerning nature and asked for more information which to many would be perceived as nosey, but for me it was therapeutic.

By this time, I had become so comfortable disclosing my soul, that my seat which was once positioned close to the exit door of the office, was now positioned right in front of his desk in which my hands were resting.

"I made it a habit to run into my husband's arms after a long day of work just to show him how much I missed him and at a point, he actually welcomed me with open arms. Lately, it appears that my presence only frustrates him forcing him to yell as I am seen coming near. We have not slept in the same bed for over a month now and the only time in which intercourse transpires is when he is in the mood and honestly it is very sparingly. The biggest issue of all is the fact that I have mentioned starting a family and he has declined each time the topic presents itself. Before we got married, we dreamed of starting a family, now that we are finally husband and wife the conversation sparks a huge argument that I have to walk away from as if the desire to have a family with my husband is morally wrong. I honestly feel like I am becoming a burden to him and that he has possibly fallen out of love with me. Now I'm playing the waiting game and wondering when he is going to open up and tell me so that I can stop guessing what the root of the problem truly is."

After wrapping up my vent to Timothy, I myself blew out a sigh of relief. I could not believe that I had said so much and in doing so, I also could not help, but wonder what his feelings were about my personal life now that I had exposed much of it. We stared at each other for a brief moment, myself waiting for a response from Timothy and I believe he waited to see if there was anything else I wanted to get off my chest.

Neither party stepping up to the plate to converse, Timothy cleared his throat, leaned forward, and with a look of satisfaction, opened up and said, "Thank you!"

Squinting my eyes, uncertain of why he was thanking me, I knew that there had to be more to follow such a random expression of gratitude and awaited to hear what would proceed.

With his hands held together in prayer position, Timothy placed them in front of his mouth and extended them in my direction, "From what you just shared and the emotion following each and every word spoken, I could tell that this was hidden pain you had not disclosed to anyone and I thank you for trusting me."

Without another word, Timothy appeared in front of me and cuffed his right hand underneath my chin, speaking fulfilling words that I had never heard from anyone else, "Lesley you are beautiful. Never allow anyone to steal your happiness. I'm here for you whenever you need a shoulder to cry on or someone who will just be there to listen."

This man that appeared before me seemed completely genuine in his words. Other than the touch to my chin which startled me a bit, he had not used my pain as leverage to come on to me or cross any boundary which I initially feared he may.

He saw to it that my car was fixed in a timely manner and charged me next to nothing for repairs that totaled well over four hundred dollars. He even sent out for lunch which was shared in his office all while keeping the remainder of our conversation PG.

As the mechanic paged in that my car was fixed, I collected any waste from my lunch and thanked him yet again for being there in more ways than one, "Timothy thank you for today. It is much appreciated. I've never cried in front of anyone and I am grateful to you for not forming any opinions on my dysfunctional marriage."

Just as I walked over towards the trash can to dispose of my container, Timothy grabbed it to dispose himself and asked one final question of the day, "Would you please start calling me Tim? The only person that calls me Timothy is my grandmother."

This request was one that I did not have to contemplate honoring for he had a name preference and out of respect, I agreed. "I think I can handle that Timothy. I mean Tim."

We both laughed as we prepared to exit his office.

He opened the door and walked me out to the front entrance where my car awaited and made certain to beat me to the driver side where he opened the door for me. Not only did he have the tech repair all areas of my car that were in need of fine tuning, but he had them wash it and detail the inside free of charge which I certainly was not expecting.

"You be careful Miss Lesley and thank you for the conversation today. Like I said, text me if you ever need to talk. Sometimes the shop gets crazy and I have to step in and service cars myself which makes it hard for me to respond in a timely fashion, but I promise I will always get back to you."

Just before he closed my driver side door, I reached out to shake his hand as a gesture of appreciation and happily said, "Thank you again."

I drove off overly satisfied with the service, car feeling

and smelling brand new, but also clearing the service lot with the sentiment that I had a new-found friend that I was actually comfortable confiding in. Tim wanted nothing, but to listen and be there where anyone else would only focus on their problems never once asking how I was.

I pulled up to the driveway of our home feeling rejuvenated and just as I exited out of the car after being gone for two hours, I crossed paths with Trent on our front porch who continued to speed walk by without a hug, kiss, or inquiry about my service experience. Instead, he shouted from his car not to wait up for him wearing a tailored suit smelling of the Armani cologne that I had purchased for his birthday.

As much as I wanted to question Trent's whereabouts on a Saturday afternoon with such a distinct scent and exterior presentation, I laid my emotions by the wayside and proceeded on with my afternoon. This consisted of lounging upstairs watching TV alone as I always did unless I found myself buried in office work that I had to bring home. To waste what turned out to be a good afternoon festering on Trent was something I just couldn't do and so I proceeded on with my life.

Just as I connected my phone to the wall charger and made myself comfortable in the bed, I received a message from

Tim that read, "You're simply beautiful!"

Talk about a pick me up message. Yet again, Tim always knew the right moment to cheer me up and thanks to his timing, my night would end well also.

CHAPTER SEVEN

NO ROOM TO REPAIR

I woke up thanking God this morning for allowing me to see twenty-four years of life. He had gotten me through so much with the loss of my mother and father six months apart and the trying times with my husband attempting to keep our marriage afloat. Sometimes I felt that I had no one to turn to even more after losing my parents, but God always answered my prayers and for this, I could rejoice and say thank you on my birthday.

The day started entering into work to find a few surprises from personnel. The office had put together a morning brunch in celebration of my special day and had even gone as far as decorating my desk with balloons and streamers. The breakfast spread was delicious and my cake was truly beautiful. I received a bouquet of flowers which held a fifty-dollar Starbucks card that all staff members chipped in and purchased.

It was such a great feeling to be loved and appreciated

by my coworkers and if I were being catered to like this here at work, I could only imagine what festivities my husband had in stored once I arrived home this evening.

Scheduling myself a half day because I had much on my agenda before arriving home, I was honored to share the afternoon with the lovely Stacy who had surprised me with a spa package for two. Never having received a massage before, I was excited to not only embark on this experience, but to also have some girl time with Stacy and from the way that she dragged around the office with a blank stare on her face as if her mind were in the clouds, I could tell that she needed some relaxation as well.

After cutting the first slice of cake and opening a few more gifts from fellow coworkers, Stacy and I were off on a pampering retreat.

Upon checking in for our one o'clock reservation, Stacy and I were instructed to head to the changing room where we were to remove all articles of clothing and dress in a white robe before reporting to the masseuse station. While changing, I could not help, but notice that Stacy was as quiet as a mouse. Even if something were bothering her, the emotions would have revealed themselves by now and since they had not and this was supposed to be a relaxing afternoon in celebration of me, I tried not to read too much into her distance and escorted myself to the massage table allowing Stacy to join on her own accord.

Feeling calm and relaxed at the hands of a masseuse who was gently removing the tension from my body, I was more than thankful to Stacy for providing me with such a gift that I wanted to express my gratitude, "Thank you for the massage Stacy. You have no idea how bad I needed this."

Her response went right along with her demeanor. It was forced as if she were under duress, "Sure."

By this point, I felt that Stacy was signaling a cry for help and as much as I wanted to remain in a state of positive energy, I just couldn't leave my girl hanging so as always, I placed my feelings on the back burner and entered into investigative mode.

With only a thin linen sheet separating our beds as form of privacy, I turned my cheek over in her direction so that I could unravel her somewhat lost focus, "What's going on Stacy? You don't seem like you're enjoying yourself."

Whatever he had done this time, I'm sure that it could

not have been worse than the damage already caused which one would assume she would be numb to at this point.

I could hear a muffled sniffle come from Stacy and knew that the words would trail right behind as I had given the invitation to vent from across the room which she indirectly asked for, "Last night he told me that he wasn't in love with me anymore."

Finally. Maybe now Stacy would have the necessary closure that would force her to move on and notice her true worth. I mean, it is not that I was happy that her husband revealed that the love was gone, but maybe this would further explain his cheating ways and force Stacy to just walk away from any further embarrassment. Even I myself wished that Trent would open up and let me know if the love was there because at this point all I could do was assume that it was gone on his end. At least in Stacy's position, she finally knew where her marriage stood and hopefully this disclosure would set her free.

"Do you think he meant it?"

The one thing I had learned about love was the fact that your best friend, mother, father, cousin, niece, nephew, even pastor could tell you all day long that you deserved better, but until you actually believed it mind, body, and soul, words did not mean a thing which is why I didn't even bother telling Stacy that she could do better. Instead, I played along until she told me how this conversation came to be.

"Was this out of anger? What would make him say this out of the blue?"

I could hear footsteps coming over in my direction and as I looked up, Stacy appeared removing the sheet that divided us so that she could signal for me to walk across the room with her. I too joined, excusing myself from the calming massage I was indulging in as we needed a private moment away from anyone else that was near. We walked over to a small lounging area that had three chairs and a table that were unoccupied and talked about last night's events which led to the seemingly painful revelation.

Stacy leaned her head back on the wall and rubbed her face from top to bottom with both palms opened and took me on a journey inside of her previous evening, "I had come in the house with the mail and a hand-written letter was addressed to my husband which I originally placed on our kitchen table like I would with any other piece of mail addressed to him.

After sitting on the couch for over an hour waiting on my husband to walk through the door, my curiosity would not take focus away from the pink envelope and so I waited no more."

If Stacy was getting ready to tell me that he had fathered yet another child, I was going to stand before her, tell her all the feelings that I kept bottled inside for sake of not hurting her, and cut our ladies afternoon short. I was not going to listen to this same broken record anymore and sat at the edge of my seat in possible route of the exit.

"Did you ever open the letter?"

She pulled a pink envelope out of the side pocket of her robe and began to lift the flap that was folded inside. Due to her preparedness, I was starting to feel as though our ladies outing was a platform for Stacy to vent all along and not a true celebration of my birthday as her friend. Slightly irritated, I waited for her to open the contents of the actual letter itself trying not to get offended about how this afternoon had turned out.

"Daddy, thank you for spending the night with me and your son. I'm glad that you are finally making an effort to be in Jr's life as this is all that I have asked."

Jasmine Herring's, *More Than Enough*

Stacy looked up at me with a sight of disgust, but so far the letter appeared harmless. I mean, I would not have addressed a married man as daddy, but maybe she was writing from her child's perspective. I mean after all, Stacy had accepted the children he already fathered and accepting the children also meant accepting their mothers her husband had cheated with.

"Does the letter say anything else?"

Thinking that this was the basis of the letter, I gave Stacy's husband and the mother of his child the benefit of the doubt. As if I were being dismissive of the words written, Stacy looked at me with eyes of fury as though I had switched sides and partnered up with the female who had written the letter before continuing on.

"Watching you rock our son to sleep made me feel like I had the perfect family. You take such great care of our son and I'm thankful that he has you in his life. You could have left after laying our son down, but instead you also laid me down and well. The love making that transpired between the two of us showed me that you still care and I do too. Although you did not tell me that you were married until after our son was conceived, I cannot deny my love for you. I hope that in time, we can give our love a second try for the sake of our son, but until that happens, I will wait on you. Love, the mother of your one and only son."

I prayed that Stacy could not see my jaw which had fallen flat on the floor upon conclusion of her ending such a bold letter. I could not even look into her eyes for I too was shocked by a piece of mail that began as an innocent thank you and quickly turned into an intimate recount with future dreams to follow.

"What did your husband say when you showed him the letter? You did confront him, right?"

Stacy delicately folded the letter and placed it back in the side pocket of her terrycloth robe as if it were some sort of souvenir. It wasn't clear to me why she was holding on to this letter and maybe she would explain as she began to answer one of my many questions.

"I asked him if he had slept with her and he began yelling, first accusing me of screening his mail and then telling me that I always accuse him of sleeping around. He said that because of me, our relationship was failing and that if it ended, I would only have myself to blame. Just before storming out of the house and slamming the front door, he told me that he was falling out of love with me and that I was too insecure to be anyone's wife."

There were simply no words that I could extend to make light of the situation. I truly believed that Stacy was growing tired of dealing with the same turmoil and possibly ready to let it all go.

With such a low blow learning that her husband was still in fact sleeping around, although she did shed a tear or two, they were nothing like those I had seen before. This time they were faint and not pouring from her face which to me was a sign that Stacy was coming towards the shedding of her last and final tears.

Not wanting to dwell on anymore foolishness nor bad news, I decided to cut our massages short and invite her to the salon with me as I was getting highlights for the first time. My husband was always going crazy over the women he had seen on television with color in their hair and I thought I would surprise him by getting some myself. I only hoped that this change would not backfire and that my alter ego would turn him on. I invited Stacy because she needed to be around good vibes and laughter and my stylist was just the one to get the job done. I even went a step further and offered to pay for her to get her hair done as well as I did not want her to simply watch me. Hopefully this would cheer her up and make her feel a little more alive.

After massages, the salon, lunch, and getting our nails done, Stacy and I went our separate ways for the evening as I had to make my grand entrance home to see what my husband had cooking up for my birthday. I contemplated stopping by the grocery store, but uncertain of what Trent had prepared, I decided not to step on his toes and just head home, this time at a decent hour which I'm sure he would approve.

Nervous about what he would think of my hair as he had no notion that it was being done, I pulled into our driveway and walked in the front door with the hood from my jacket covering my head until I was in plain view of my husband.

I walked in to our home very observant and the first thing my eyes laid sight on was a stack of mail on our credenza containing four birthday cards from family members. As my sense of smell was not triggered, I walked into the kitchen opening the oven and noticed that nothing had been prepared which led me to believe that we were possibly going out for dinner. With no luck searching downstairs for Trent, I could soon hear footsteps up the stairs and with his car still in the driveway, I knew that he was home, hopefully in a good mood ready to have some fun.

Anxiously walking up the stairs, hood still remaining over my head and birthday cards in hand, I entered into our bedroom where Trent could be found getting dressed.

I stood in front of him all smiles, hoping that he would get the clue and possibly remove the hood from my head, but instead his sarcasm introduced its ugly face, "Why do you have that silly hood on your head?"

I answered his question through action and slowly revealed the finished product of my hair while combing my fingers through the static areas awaiting Trent's response whether that be verbal or visual, "what do you think Trent?"

Second guessing whether or not I should have asked what he thought, Trent took a brief moment to examine my hair front to back and walked into the closet giving not even a one sentence response. Assuming that he was not impressed by my hair change, I plopped myself on the bed where I second guessed what I had just done to my hair.

Still awaiting a reaction, Trent exited the closet, took

one look at his phone and threw it down on the bed right next to me. Uncertain of what he had just seen on his phone, Trent began pacing back and forth from the bedroom to the bathroom as if he had somewhere to be with little time to spare. Maybe he did love my change, but his limited time would not allow him to focus on my hair. Whether or not that was the truth, I was going to run with It.

Not yet receiving an invitation, I too took the initiative to get dressed as I saw Trent doing the same. I was ecstatic and could not wait to begin my birthday celebration with my husband no longer questioning if he was going to verbally tell me happy birthday or not. My guess was that he had so many things planned that he was just too focused and needed me to hurry up.

After hopping in and out of the shower, I invaded my side of the closet on a mission to find the perfect outfit that would go with my new and improved hair. I searched high and low and placed my eyes on the sexiest black form fitting dress that had a hint of gold trim at the neck line which went perfect with my honey brown highlights.

While I got dressed, Trent took a stroll down the stairs where his phone remained on the bed and began to vibrate. I shouted out for him to come and get his phone as I was not the type of wife to invade his privacy. Failing to respond to my call, I proceeded to pick up the phone just to make certain that his job was not in need of his assistance. Once I grabbed the phone to take it to Trent who remained downstairs in an area that I could not be heard, I did not have to pry for the sender's message could be seen through the screen which read, "Meet at Strip Club Uno, 523 Cherry Lake Rd."

After reading the text, I realized that Trent was not dressed for me and that my birthday was going to be spent alone. Refraining from tearing up, I walked outside to find Trent who was wiping down his car with a rag and handed him his phone. I was disappointed in myself for actually believing Trent would be any different simply because it was my birthday.

"Here Trent. Your phone was going off."

As much as I wanted to throw the phone at Trent's head for watching me get dressed knowing that he was not courting me as his wife around the town, I thought twice for fear of an assault charge as well as a tarnished reputation around the neighborhood.

You would think that holding my composure would

keep Trent from chiming off, but instead somehow, he managed to turn the tables on me for he believed that I was invading his phone privacy.

"Why are you touching my phone anyway?"

I had only brought his phone downstairs because it was going off and did not want him to miss an important call. Not once had I ever looked through his phone the entire time it lay next to me where he threw it in the first place and now he was mad at me because obviously, he had something to hide.

Removing all accessories from my body including the earrings from each lobe now knowing that this night was not about me, I responded to his accusations, "You left your phone next to me. I only touched it to bring it to you."

Trent snatched the phone out of my hand and continued on his rampage, "Why are you taking your earrings off like we're about to box with one another? You need to calm your ass down."

It was bad enough that I dealt with this form of attack on a day to day basis, but on my birthday, I expected a day of peace and already I had dealt with Stacy's misery and now Trent was attacking me. Some birthday I was having.

"Trent. I thought that you and I were going out this evening."

Reaching my limit, I stepped up close to his face and ended the conversation, "Seeing as though you have other plans, I have no reason to keep my earrings in. That's why I am taking them off."

His facial expression made it clear that he had no idea what today was or what would bring me to think we had any type of plans, "What is so special today that made you put color in your hair and wear that tight ass dress?"

We were too young to be forgetful, but here my husband was not knowing that I had done all of this because it was my birthday; his wife's birthday.

"Today is my birthday Trent."

Stating nothing or even displaying an ounce of remorse as I revealed why I had gone through so much trouble today to doll myself up, Trent ran back inside of the house where he brought out his car keys and set me straight about this one particular day that I thought I should be made to feel special. "This is just another day Lesley. Take that dress off and save it for another time. I'm not sure when I will be home tonight so don't wait up."

He gave me a drive by kiss to my cheek with his lips just barely touching my face and that was the last that I saw of Trent that evening. My family was so big on celebrations and here I was married to a man who found birthday's to be just another day. If my parents were here, they would have planned a surprise party as they did each year and had gifts awaiting my arrival. Without them, birthdays just weren't the same.

I wished that I had listened to my gut instinct when I thought to go to the grocery store because there was nothing in the house to eat as I was anticipating a nice romantic dinner. Instead, I found myself ordering a pizza, watching Netflix, and playing on my phone.

My diary was definitely deserving of an entry this evening on what a joyous day I had celebrating my birthday. I had the entire house to myself and with no plans, I could write away not looking over my shoulder for Trent to appear.

I could hear my phone signal that I had an unread text message while downstairs with the delivery man and just as I closed the door with the dinner I was forced to eat, I walked up the stairs to check my phone and the text message read,

"Thinking of you Miss Lesley!"

It was Tim and as much as he had been there when I needed someone, he was not the person that I needed at the moment; my husband was. Not wanting to be rude, I responded to his message hoping that he would get the hint that tonight was not a good night to play knight in shining armor, "Thanks."

I was not trying to be mean, but I was furious and upset at the way my day turned out and could not see a conversation with another man bringing positive energy. All I wanted was to feel loved and instead I felt unappreciated and unwanted. I just couldn't see Tim's conversation making me feel any better and the thought of him being the one reaching out was unsettling.

Sure enough, as much as I wanted to push Tim away, he responded yet again questioning the unmoving response I had given, "Are you ok?"

I could tell that his persistence wasn't going to let up. Did I want to tell him what was bothering me? I did not want him to just see me as this emotional victim in need of sympathy, but lately that's all that I was. With no one else to talk to, I thought what the hell and released my feelings, fearless of any response he would give in return. Tim opened the door for me to vent and I took it full speed.

"My husband forgot my birthday today. I colored my hair and came home hoping that he had something special planned for me only for him to tell me that he was on his way out the door. Once I reminded him that it was my birthday, he was neither apologetic nor willing to drop his plans. He said that this was just another day and we would do something later. I'm just a bit down at the moment as this day has not been made to feel special at all."

It had been ten minutes since I had sent the response letting Tim in on my not so pleasant day and with no response in return I made the assumption that he was tired of hearing my cry out and as I was tired of being the one to cry out, I placed my phone on the charger and expected to hear nothing back from Tim whom I had probably run off by now.

Just as my body began the process of dozing off while watching a movie, I received a response from Tim and with him taking so long to respond, I read with caution.

The text message was full of birthday emoji in celebration of me. He had selected a picture of a cake, three flowers, balloons, and a pair of heels. The images were then proceeded by words, "This is not just another day for this is the day to celebrate the life of an amazingly beautiful woman. I'm sorry that he could not see that. This day is special because you are special Lesley. Pick any day this week and I would love to treat you to lunch."

Why couldn't this message come from my husband? The best gift of my entire day did not cost a penny nor did it cause for much thought. It was the kind words stated by a person who still till this day did not speak negatively about my pain, but continued to lift me up at my weakest moments.

I just could not understand how a person who barely knew me saw fit to be there for me and notice the small detail while the person I had spent years building a life with was withering away and disregarding each and every attempt to save our marriage.

It was time to speak with my husband because this distance between us could no longer continue. I had to tell him how I felt for I was starting to believe that our marriage was in true jeopardy and if not saved soon, there may be no room left for repair.

CHAPTER EIGHT

DO IT THEN

It was five in the morning and yet Trent still had not made it in the house. After calling him repeatedly, receiving no answer, I became worried and decided to brew a pot of coffee to keep myself awake long enough to determine my next course of action.

Having never stepped foot in one, I was almost certain that strip clubs did not remain open this late, but tried hard to only focus on my husband's safe arrival and not the events of last night which left me lonely.

By six a.m., trying his phone one last time with no response, I decided to run upstairs, throw on a pair of sweats, and go out searching for my husband whom I was now fearful for.

Just before heading out of the door, I made sure to turn the pot of coffee off and pour myself a tall thermal glass as I was only half awake. I gathered my wallet and keys and as I was heading out of the door, placed my first call to the nearest hospital to see if my husband had been admitted.

I remained on the front porch long enough for the receptionist to search her records for my husband's name and while on hold, out of nowhere, Trent decided to pull into the driveway just barely missing the mailbox he almost took off of its post.

Not sure whether to yell, I ended the call with the hospital receptionist and decided to wait and see what state Trent was in before going any further.

I literally watched this man practically crawl from the car to the front porch while holding on to his cellphone and yet he could not answer my calls to let me know that he was ok. Without a word, he slouched over behind me and rubbed my head like I was a small puppy or infant child being embraced just before walking inside of the house.

As much as I wanted to leave him alone until he sobered up, I could not help, but to detect perfume all over his clothing as he leaned towards me. He had some explaining to do, questions to answer, and what better time to get the truth out than while he was still drunk.

Chugging down the entire pot of coffee, I remained in close enough distance to watch my husband drag around the house slurring his words and I knew that now was a better time than ever for the intervention that our marriage desperately needed.

I sat at our kitchen table and waited for Trent to finish the coffee I had brewed so that he could join me for a marital discussion, "Trent, would you come sit with me for a moment please. We need to talk."

With no hesitation, Trent stumbled over towards me, pulled the chair from underneath the kitchen table, and sat in it backwards with an unpleasant appearance.

I looked into his eyes that were glossy and blood shot red and waited no longer to voice my concerns.

"Did you see that I called you?"

Looking at me with a blank stare, he responded, "which time?"

Who was this man sitting before me because he

certainly was not my husband, but a total stranger who had taken his place.

"How could you stay out this late and not even bother to call? I was worried that something happened to you."

I was so frustrated at this point for more reasons than one. It was bad enough that our marriage had taken a turn in the wrong direction, but Trent's actions lately were not making things any better and I was not certain if he even cared. Remaining quiet, I waited to see if Trent was going to fess up to his whereabouts or any action for that matter. Hell, I just wanted him to say something.

He began to doze off in front of me due to his drunkenness, but the issues had to be addressed which is why I tried to keep him with me in conversation, "Trent you have come in this house after six a.m., reeking of both alcohol and perfume. What is going on with you?"

Rising from his chair, I could sense that Trent was getting upset and if he did not verbally express his anger, throwing the dining room chair to the ground made it obvious.

Nowhere near finished with my conversation and receiving no answers to my questions, Trent took his anger over into the living room where he turned the television on and tuned me out making this a failed intervention.

I called Trent's name from in the kitchen where I remained alone, pleading with him to come and finish our discussion, but he ignored my cries continuing to watch TV. Tapping my nails on the dining room table for a few moments, I made the decision to rise from the chair and if Trent was not going to come to me, I was surely heading over in his direction.

Walking over towards the living room, I could see that the remote was held loosely in Trent's hands and with his reflexes not in the best shape due to his drunken state, I snatched the remote control from his hand and turned off the TV which did not go over well.

"What the fuck are you doing," shouted Trent.

It took all of this to gain his attention and I was not about to lose it. He could curse all he wanted to, but he was damn sure going to listen.

Sitting in close proximity of Trent, I stated my position as he so disrespectfully inquired, "I have asked you twice to sit and talk to me because you need to hear this. The television can wait." I reached over, tugging on Trent's shirt, lifting the collar

Jasmine Herring's, *More Than Enough*

up to his nose and asked with no remorse, "Who did the perfume come from?"

Frustration high as if I was the one causing problems, Trent attempted to stand before me and reach for the remote. He probably could have retrieved it had it not been for being off balance. Due to his immobile state he could do nothing, but yell and act irrational all while glued to the couch.

"Why does it matter whose perfume is on me? I came home right?"

Was I supposed to be grateful that he came home in the condition that he was in and simply ignore the red flags? Did this man think that I was going to stand for disrespect? It was time to diminish the arrogance and put my foot down, "What you will not do is disrespect me and ignore my calls especially when I am trying to make sure that you are ok. What you also won't do is come home whenever you feel like it as if you are not a married man. Third and foremost, you will never in your life come back to the home we share, smelling of women's perfume. Do you hear what I am saying to you Trent?"

I hated speaking to him this way for this was not my character at all, but this seemed to be the only form of communication that he understood and I was running out of options to get my point across.

Laughing nonstop, I could not tell if it was the alcohol, something was funny to Trent, or he was making fun of my delivery, but I waited for him to make light of his current behavior.

Barely able to lift from his position on the couch, Trent stood in my face where every glass of Vodka could be detected through his breath and called himself checking me in his own way, "If I want to stay out, I'm going to stay out. If I don't want to answer your damn calls, deal with it. As far as the perfume goes, as I said, I come home to you, don't I?"

This had been the second time that Trent had disregarded the scent of perfume and excused it by stating that he comes home to me. Was this an admission of possible cheating? I wasn't trying to draw any conclusions, but out of our entire relationship, not once had I ever suspected or accused him of cheating until now and I wasn't sure how to deal with it.

"Trent, do you even want to be a part of this marriage any longer?"

Remaining in my face, Trent looked at me with a smirk and walked away grabbing his car keys off of the kitchen table.

I had devoted my life to this man and I was not going to stand by and watch our marriage go down the drain without a fight even if I was fighting alone. I ran towards the front door where Trent was preparing to exit in effort to stop him and ask a few more questions.

"Trent. How would you feel if I came home whenever I chose to? How would you feel if I entered our home smelling of another man's cologne?"

Attempting to bypass me and walk out of the door, I grabbed a hold of Trent's right arm, forcing him to remain and look at me with my fingers positioning his chin. "How would you feel?"

I wanted him to show me that he cared and this was my ultimate plea. Right here and right now I needed answers about our marriage and some sign that it was not coming to an end.

"Lesley, you aren't going anywhere. Move so I can leave."

That was one of the major problems. He never thought I was capable of letting go and moving forward. Sure, I had threatened to leave before, but never had I proved to Trent that I was serious which is why up until now, he had a valid claim.

Tears began to flow from my eyes because my husband could not understand that I was crying for help for the both of us and wasn't being met half way. I stated one final revelation while trying hard to hold back any further tears, "Maybe I should see what else is out there for me."

Had that admission really come from my mouth? With my emotions high and feelings destroyed, I was consumed at an all-time high that I just didn't know what else to say.

Not sure if he heard me or was taking time to process my words, Trent walked out of the house, pushing through me like a linebacker on the football field and headed towards the car not saying a single word.

"Did you hear me Trent? What if I want to see what else is out there for me?

Remaining in the doorway, feeling broken at the words that I had just stated, I watched my husband walk away and at this point I was not sure if he were hurt, upset, or signaling that he was done with our marriage.

Just as I turned to walk inside of the house and close the front door, Trent shouted from inside of his car very hostile, "Do it then Lesley," reversed out of the driveway and sped away.

I watched my husband fade into the clouds, unwilling to fight for our marriage and you know what, the position he had put me in, I was not sure if I was capable of fighting alone any longer. Never had I imagined my marriage coming to this point. All I could do was walk in the house, shut the front door, and either close this chapter of my life or accept the things that I obviously had no control over.

CHAPTER NINE

WHO HAS MY BACK

Two weeks had gone by since shedding light on Trent that I was unhappy and still, no effort on his part had taken place to make me feel any different than I did about our marital differences. With the distance growing stronger between the two of us, I could not help, but question whether or not I should seek some form of advisement on my option to separate. I certainly did not want to take this course of action, but Trent had been separated from me for so long at this point that it was unfair to remain all alone. If he could not fight for us, what reason did I have to stay?

Each passing day felt lonelier as Trent was coming home less and less. The dinner table in which I always rushed home to set, was only occupied by one and the bedroom was the coldest in the entire house.

When Trent did manage to come home, I found no need to question his whereabouts or attack his lack of respect as a married man for it was clear that he had made his choice.

Whoever or whatever was keeping my husband away was clearly able to give him something that I just could not and I was starting to come to peace with my decision to dissolve our marriage. There was no longer any reason to fuss or fight which was the problem with many relationships including Stacy's. Too much time was wasted arguing and going back and forth about who did what and why. When you know deep down in your heart that you have done all that you can, you have to make the decision to let go for if not, you are practically settling.

I was preparing to walk away from years invested and mistake not, this was extremely painful to me as I grew up with loving parents who personified a solid relationship, but I was not going to be walked over nor settle for less than I deserved and I knew that I deserved more than this.

I never saw myself reaching this point in my marriage and it was hard dealing with the knowledge that I had no one that I could confide in. The workplace was not the platform to vent and my closest friend Stacy was far from the person I would ever take advice from when it came to men and relationships. The only person I could think to speak with was Tim who was of the opposite sex and could give me a male's perspective, the problem was, I had since been avoiding him.

It wasn't that he had done anything wrong per say, but he displayed a charismatic demeanor that made me uncomfortable. It was extremely coincidental that he always made his presence known at my darkest moments and when responding and letting him in whatever was going on at the time, his persistence forced him to step in and attempt to take my problems away which I just could not understand. Why did he even care? I mean, who would want to continuously speak with a married female consumed by numerous problems? I just could not figure Tim out and hoped that by my distancing myself and not responding to his text messages or taking my car in since the first repair that he would just go away, but boy was I wrong.

Since my birthday, he had tried to invite me over to the office for lunch trying to make up for what my husband failed to do which I firmly declined; another reason I chose to distance myself. I could not spell out any other way that I was married and he needed to get that through his head and remain in the place of a mechanic only. Part of me felt as though he saw an open invitation to swoop in and save the day as I had let him in on some of my troubles, which I was starting to regret, and if that was the case, he was mistaken. Maybe there were married women out there that he was used to courting through their despair who may welcome him with open arms, but I was not one of them. I took my vows seriously despite the tough road ahead.

The only friend left to confide in and would pass no judgement was my lovely little diary whom I had been neglectful towards as I was becoming more vocal with Trent and a lot less quiet. If no one else had my back, I knew that I could count on my diary and she and I had some serious catching up to do for I had yet to introduce Tim.

ONE STEP TOO CLOSE

Stranded on the side of the road with a flat tire, I contemplated flagging down someone driving by, but realized how dangerous that could be. Then it dawned on me that there were two people I could ask for assistance despite not wanting to; my husband Trent who was practically MIA in my life or Tim whom I kept my distance for reasons of my own. Waving down a stranger was looking more and more like a better option, but seeing as though I did not want to fall victim to the most recent homicide ending up with the wrong person, I had to toughen up and make a decision on who to contact. It was either Trent, full of mind games who may or may not show, or Tim who had flirtatious ways and seemed to want so much more than to just assist me with car repairs.

With nowhere important to travel, I sat weighing my pros and cons until it was decided who I would run to in the time of need.

Dialing each number as slow as possible making certain that I had made the right decision, the first ring sounded and I awaited an answer. Not even two complete rings and here I was nervous at the sound of his voice. To my surprise, he appeared calm and opened up our line of communication in a friendly manner putting my nerves at slight ease, "Well hello. It's been a minute."

Yes, I chose to call Tim only because I knew that with this route there would no yelling, I told you so, or a lengthy period before help arrived if it did at all.

As much as I wanted to get straight to the point as to my reason for calling, I learned that it was rude not to greet a person properly and so I treated the conversation as if Tim and I were best friends who had known each other our entire lives, "Hey Tim! How are you?"

Hoping that he would ignore the distance that had been kept between us on account of myself, I continued in search of possible shortness in conversation or slight anger that would indicate the possibility that he may not come to my aid, but the more we talked, the less worried I became as his attitude remained positive with each response he delivered, "I can't complain. How is the lovely Lesley doing on this fine afternoon?"

Could he just stop with the compliments and allow me to speak? Yet another reason I thought twice about contacting him as I did not want to open any door. "I'm actually stranded on the side of the road with a flat tire. Do you have anyone nearby that could come and fix it or at least put the spare on for me?"

Tim's words were replaced with loud clanging as if he had a pair of keys in his hand and the next thing I knew, I could hear a car engine start and Keith Sweat's song *Twisted* playing in the background. I was not sure if Tim was returning the favor of ignoring me or working on a car in which I was now feeling like an inconvenience, wondering if I should disregard my request.

By no means was I using him which I hoped that he knew as well. I looked at this call as a business transaction; one in which compensation would be exchanged upon completion of service. I only hoped that Tim knew this as well and was not contemplating on whether or not to come to my aid.

Had he forgotten that I was on the phone, "Tim? Are you still there?" I could hear the music lower in volume and now I awaited a response as to whether or not help was on the way, "I'm in the car now. Where are you exactly?"

Wow. This man just stopped all that he was doing and hopped in the car to help me with no further questions asked? It wasn't more than ten minutes after calling and disclosing my exact location that Tim was parked right behind my car, crouched down on the ground to investigate my tire.

Entrusting me with his own personal car keys, Tim had allowed me to sit in his car so that I would not have to stand on my feet waiting. It was in his car I remained still and silent observing his workmanship. Upon arrival, Tim had not brought up the fact that he had checked in on me from time to time receiving no response.

I got out of the car feeling terribly guilty for my behavior towards him and interrupted the repair by asking if there was anything that I could do to help out which he declined. Not knowing what else to say as his conversation was short, I got back in his car and helped myself to a little personal investigation of my own. Touching none of his personal items nor going in to any closed compartment, with my eyes only, I looked around to learn a little more about this mysterious man who was ever kind in gesture.

For a male he was pretty neat. I mean with Trent, there were wrappers all over the floor along with office work that he never kept organize in a briefcase nor folder despite having all of the above. Tim was well organized with not an item out of place. The only interior information that I gathered from his car other than the fact that he practiced cleanliness was that he chewed double mint gum and wore Versace cologne which I did help myself to smell and boy did it take my senses somewhere.

Indulging in the cologne longer than I should, I did not notice Tim approaching his vehicle causing my reaction to drop the lid on the floor. By the time he had opened the driver side door, the cologne remained in my hand and I felt as though I had some explaining to do as I held his belongings.

Completely embarrassed I apologized, "I'm so sorry. I just wondered what it smelled like."

Smiling as usual, Tim sat in the driver seat, undressing me with his eyes, and asked, "Well what do you think of the smell?"

Thank God he had a sense of humor because I did not want him to think that I was snooping around. "Very nice."

While discussing the cologne I had finally placed back into its appropriate area, I could not help, but notice that my flat tire had yet to be replaced. This struck my curiosity and wanting not to come off ungrateful, I asked the status of the repair, "Is everything ok with the tire?"

I did not mean to rush him, but we had been here twenty minutes and I was still stranded on the side of the road.

Looking in the direction of my car and then on his phone, Trent explained the reason behind the stall, "There is a burr on the tire that is hindering me from removing it in order to replace it. I contacted one of my tow men and he is on the way to take it back to my shop where we will get it fixed in no time."

Before I could respond, out of nowhere, my stomach began to growl which was so embarrassing. Preparing to catch the next sound that may stem from my stomach, I wrapped my arms tightly around my belly and apologized for the outburst, "I'm sorry about that."

Staring at his phone, Tim mentioned that it was about lunch time and asked if I were hungry as he knew of a great diner up the road. Even though I was hungry as if my stomach hadn't given that information out, we had already had this conversation a million and one times and just because he was fixing my tire did not mean I was going to cave in this time. Lunch was not on the agenda especially in a public setting where anyone who knew me could speculate and/or run back to Trent with false information. If anything, I was going to ride back to the shop with the tow man and wait in the lobby like any other customer.

"No thank you. I'm fine."

Just as Tim was about to fix his lips to respond to my decline of lunch, through the rearview mirror I could see the tow man who could not have come at a more perfect time making my escape from Tim a little easier, "If you don't mind, I will ride back with the tow man."

With a quickness, Tim turned in his seat to face me just as I was preparing to open the front passenger side door and spoke with eyes of confusion, "It's just lunch Lesley. I won't do anything to disrespect you. It's a small diner up the road and we can even get the food to go if that makes you feel more comfortable. Come on your stomach already told on you."

Here I was with my entire right hand on the handle of the door slowly loosening my grip as I began to feel obligated to have lunch. I mean, he did stop what he was doing to come to my rescue and he was trying his best to make me feel more comfortable. I was hungry and if we did order to go like he said,

I guess it wouldn't hurt and so I agreed, but only on the condition that he went in and got the food and that we took it back to the shop which he accepted my terms.

After writing down my order, Tim entered into the diner making this the perfect opportunity to contact Trent. Part of my conscience was telling me that I should not be in this situation nor out with another man even if innocent. With the call going straight to voicemail not sure if I was being ignored, I left a message just to let him know that he was on my mind, "Trent. I hope that your day at work is going well. I love you and will see you at home."

I would have said that I would see him this afternoon or evening, but with Trent's recent patterns, evenings were turning in to following mornings so I honestly never knew when to expect him home.

Placing our lunch in the back seat as Tim did not want me to ruin my clothes, we were headed back to the shop where my car had been sent. As we walked in through the front entrance, Tim had to make a quick detour up front at the check in desk to sign off on a few work orders. While waiting, a tech who I had seen on my first visit stopped to greet me, "How are you today Miss Lesley?"

I wasn't sure how he remembered my name and then wondered if Tim had anything to do with the techs being so nice to me. What had he said around the office in regards to me as a client only? Not wanting to be rude, I gave a simple greeting back, questioning whether or not I should stay or go as I wanted no one to interpret the wrong idea.

Entering into the office after me, Tim appeared so excited as if he had in fact stated something to the techs, but what exactly I did not know. "Have a seat Miss. Lesley."

Sitting cautiously, I chewed on my piece of gum, rotating it from the left to right side of my mouth, no longer hungry or wanting to touch my food for that matter. A million thoughts ran through my mind and I could not help but give Tim a scolding look with both eyes as he bounced around his office pleasantly like everything was fine. Had it not been for the vibration in my purse, I would have begun the interrogation process with Tim to get to the root of what had been said around the building to make everyone embrace me in such a comforting manner as though I was the first lady.

Needing to calm down as Trent was calling, I braced my feelings and gave my undivided attention to my husband not sure where the conversation was going to go, "Hello."

Sounding as though he were being forced to communicate with me, Trent's response was nothing short of an attitude, "You called me Lesley."

Someone had to reach out seeing as though Trent was making no effort to contact me. I was getting so tired of being the bigger person, but not wanting to argue especially sitting before Tim, I let Trent know that I did not intend to bother him, only check in, "I just had not heard from you and wanted to see how you were doing. That is all Trent."

I could see Tim glancing over at me, attempting to be discrete while listening to me struggle to hold a phone conversation with the man I had been dating for four years, married less than one. Feeling as though I were being rude while sitting in Tim's office, I placed the call on speaker and sat it on Tim's desk just so he could get a glimpse of just what I dealt with at home and that none of what I had ever told him was a farfetched story.

Attempting one more time to hold a decent conversation, I proceeded with more small talk wanting to keep things light and most of all, stress free, "How is your day going Trent?"

"It was fine until you interrupted it. Do you actually want something because if not, I have things to do?"

Second guessing whether or not I should have placed the phone on speaker as Trent was now acting out, I chose to let him go so that he could continue on with whatever was occupying his time.

"Trent, I did not mean to interrupt your day. Will you be home this evening?"

I asked if he would be home so I would know whether or not it was necessary to rush home and make dinner. Although I had made up in my mind based on his actions that I was ready to separate, I had yet to act and was not giving up just yet. He was still my husband and I his wife.

Having to express the last words, Trent spoke with very little care, "Don't worry about when I'm coming home. I'll get there when I do."

The call ended and I could not yet hold my head up to make eye contact with Tim for I was rather ashamed. I felt as though I was nothing more to Trent than an old fling he was trying to get rid of. He treated me worse than any enemy and to think, part of me was still trying. I mean what was I actually holding on to?

I stood from my seat, grabbed my purse, and attempted to walk out of the door thanking Tim for his help. I had to go because I just did not want to see anyone at the moment. This so-called life was knocking me down and I just did not know what direction to turn.

Meeting me at the door, Tim closed the small crack I had opened to let myself out and reminded me that I had not eaten the lunch he had ordered and that my car was not yet drivable as it was without a functioning tire. At this moment I felt like a caged animal who was trapped needing to be set free.

With his hands nestled underneath my elbows guiding me back to the chair I deserted, Tim asked me to relax and sit, "Just sit down and relax. You don't have to go anywhere."

Placing my hand in the direction of Tim, with my words, I made clear that I was in no mood to be judged before I even thought to sit again, "Tim, if you are going to say anything negative, don't. This is what I have to deal with every day and I do not need anyone vocalizing their opinion about my life."

Looking away, Tim turned my cheek so that we were parallel of one another and with a serious look painted on his face asked, "Have I once judged you?"

Allowing my emotions to settle slightly so that I had a clearer conscience, I began to think of all of my encounters with Tim and to answer his question, no, he had not once judged my relationship with my husband. Here I was depicting Tim as this man who wanted something from me and not once had he made me feel poorly about my marriage or the deep pain that was starting to take over. He was the one and only person who had been there for me the last couple of weeks and here I was so hurt and distraught that I made him feel like he was just another person out to get me.

Emotions resurfacing, I broke into tears right in front of Tim. As hard as I was trying to hone in on my feelings, I continued to hit highs and lows directly in front of this man. One minute I was content with my circumstances and the next, I was bursting out into tears not only because of Trent's treatment, but also learning that as much as I continued to cry for someone to be there for me, the person who was, was the very person that I was shutting out of my life and him standing here today, just made the pain worse.

Out of all the times Tim had rushed to my aid, on this particular day he stood and watched. I could not tell if he had thrown in the towel as I had possibly shoved him to the side one too many times. He respectfully gave me the time that I needed to let it all out before asking a question that definitely took me by surprise, "What do you want from me Lesley?"

Taken back by that question as I felt that the roles had now reversed, I was not sure how to respond. I thought that I wanted someone to fix my tire which was the ultimate reason for this visit. Had I led him on in any way to believe that I wanted more? Was it something I said to encourage such a question? Looking back, I could not think of a time that I had led him on and if I had I was certainly prepared to apologize because those were not my intentions.

"Tim, if in any way I have led you to believe that I want more than a client relationship, I'm very sorry. I may have opened up to you a little too much, but you have been there when no one else was and I guess I felt comfortable confiding in you."

I watched this man look at me as if my response to his question was to him, bullshit. As if deep inside his mind, I was lying making me extremely uncomfortable. What more could I say?

Tim turned to the window in his office with his arms crossed and released a bomb, one in which I was not expecting, "Lesley is it not obvious that I care about you?"

Combing my fingers through my hair as this was my coping strategy in time of stressful situations, I genuinely did not know what this man wanted me to say. Why here and why now was he confessing this? I was in the worst spot in my life with my husband and this here made my life that much more chaotic.

"I text you constantly because I want to know that you are ok. I want you to know that someone actually does care about you when clearly your husband does not."

I was not comfortable discussing my husband any longer and felt that it was not Tim's place to point out what he thought of Trent. This conversation needed to end and it was time for me to leave before anything else was said, "Tim, I am not comfortable discussing the fact that you do not think my husband cares for me. I think that it's time for me to...."

Before I could get another word in, Tim interrupted me and with a forceful tone, asked for me to let him finish, "Please let me speak. When I see you, I want to hold you close and let you know that everything is ok. I cannot stand to watch you being mistreated. It kills me and as long as I have tried to hide my feelings, after hearing him on the phone, I just don't get how you can put up with it any longer. No man should ever disrespect a woman, let alone his wife."

It wasn't until Tim looked at me that reality hit that he was not my husband speaking. Each and every word stated by Tim, was what I wanted to hear from Trent, not another man. What had I done to be so deserving of these feelings he had verbally kept in while at the same time physically expressing?

If I was going to continue bringing my car to Tim's shop, I had to set him straight because I was not a participant of leading anyone on.

I walked over to Tim hoping to clear the air in a peaceful manner so both of us would walk away, both understanding what this was. He was an amazing man one in which I am sure that some woman would be proud to have and maybe had we met while I was single, we could have been something, but just thinking that way was wrong of me which is why Tim needed to understand that these feelings he possessed were not mutual on my end. I just wasn't sure how to go about telling him.

Honesty was all that I had and whether Tim liked it or not, it's what he was going to receive. Standing from my rested position, I walked over to Tim who had not once looked at me since expressing what was obviously weighing heavily on him and gathered my words hoping not to end on a bad note and walk out of his office with a person I could call a friend.

I extended my hand out to tap on his back in hopes to gain his attention. Just as he turned around, he cuffed his right arm behind my back, pulled me close, aligned his lips with mine and gave me a kiss that made my entire body immobile, unable to pull away.

My heart began to rise and although my mind was pulling back, my heart and body remained for I had not felt this way in months.

The next thing I knew, his hands were rubbing against my back and I could feel every bit of hurt, pain, and frustration exiting from my body.

"Boss, Miss Lesley's car is all set to go."

That was the wake-up call that my body needed to gain control and pull away from Tim with my hands pressed against his chest while he unlocked his arms. My breathing was off track. My heart was forcing me to stay, my mind was telling me to turn around. What had I just allowed to happen? I could not blame Tim solely as I had not declined what began as his very own advancement.

All I knew was that I had to leave and I had to leave now.

CHAPTER ELEVEN

LOYALTY LOST

I had been apart from Tim for almost six hours now and still all I could think about was the intimate kiss between the two of us. What bothered me most was as he pulled me close, I could have pulled away. Instead, I did nothing to intervene the advance only accept the invitation which I should have been strong enough to reject.

For a brief moment this kiss that I was now regretting felt so right causing me to close my eyes and drift off into a trance, but once reality set in, it dawned on me that Tim was not my husband and realized that our actions were anything, but right.

Consumed by guilt, I awaited Trent's arrival home. It was going to take a bottle of wine and courage that I was not sure I had to inform him of what I had done. I was not going to place any blame on Tim because I was the married party and it was I who should have stopped what I knew was wrong. I

Jasmine Herring's, *More Than Enough*

wanted there to be no secrets between us and felt that he deserved to know that although I had not initiated, I did partake in the kissing of another man.

While in the house my reflexes forced me to rise each time a car was heard passing by our home and glance through the living room curtains hoping that the next car would be Trent's. I had already recited the disclosure to my diary and although somewhat confident that I could confess, I feared that this revelation may speed up our separation which brought on feelings of emotion.

With a glass of wine in my left hand and phone in the other while my finger tip held the curtain open, I examined my phone making sure that the ringer was on full blast just in case Trent called to check in. This wasn't something he would normally do, but on account of my actions today, anything was possible even Trent changing up his own inconsistent routine.

While impatiently waiting on either a text, phone call, or keys to jingle outside of the door, Tim interrupted the anticipated arrival of my husband with his own personal text message. He stated that he was staying late at the shop and desperately needed to see me. He was bothered by his actions and needed me to know how sorry he was. Seeing as though I was already in over my head as I was now having to make a confession which could potentially bring my marriage to an end, I ignored him, erasing the message for I was already in enough trouble as it was. The thought of being in a confined space with Tim knowing and seeing how unpredictable he was, was a chance I was not willing to take.

The only person I needed to be around at this moment was my husband and the longer he took to come home the more my body shook in fear. As much as this needed to be a face to face interaction, if he was nowhere near home, he would have to learn of these events over the phone because I did not want to fall asleep with this indiscretion hanging over my head for I may never gather the courage to confess again.

As usual, he sent me straight to voicemail as if he were already aware of my actions or that I may have something heartbreaking to share and so I went with plan B, voicemail. I'm sure many would think that leaving a voicemail was the coward approach which it was, but it was the only option I had. Trent was neither home nor answering my calls. This way still allowed for me to confess and gave Trent time to process each and every word on his own before deciding whether or not we would remain in our marriage.

Awaiting the automated voicemail to recite Trent's seven-digit phone number, I heard a beep which signified that I was now being recorded and here was my green light to disclose all. Taking a deep breath which was the introduction to my not so pleasant message, I began to state my first word and found myself interrupted by a text message from Trent's phone which took me off the hook for a short moment, but made me question whether or not I would ever get this confession out that I had yet to start.

Reading what he had to say, I could not help, but wonder why it was that he could type complete sentences, but not hit one button and answer the phone. The deeper I got in to reading the message, the answer became clear, "Hello Lesley! This is Traci. Trent is a bit tied up at the moment. He'll call you back as soon as he can."

My selective vision had kicked in strong for out of the entire message, the only sentence that stuck out was, "This is Traci." Who in the hell was Traci and why did she have my husband's phone? Reading the sentence over and over again forced a bomb to explode in my heart. Yes we had problems like any other husband and wife and true, I did state that I wanted to see what was out there for me, but never did we discuss involving ourselves with the opposite sex let alone allowing them access to our personal possessions. This Traci must have been real special because Trent flipped out at the sight of me in the vicinity of his phone let alone holding it.

I knew right here and right now that I lost my husband forever and that he was not coming back to me in the same form. For him to have the audacity to allow another woman to communicate and inform me that they were occupied together let me know just where his loyalty lied and it was not with me.

How could Trent tell me this way that he was seeing someone else? How could he just throw away our marriage with no explanation for his most recent behaviors? Hurt would be an understatement of what I was at the moment. Confused couldn't even come close to my mental state. I had officially been placed on the roster of wives whose husbands were having an affair only my husband had the balls to let the other woman introduce herself instead of owning it himself.

Here I sat, waiting to confess to my husband what others would have kept a secret until either they were caught or buried in the grave. I toyed with the idea of responding to this Traci character and realized that she was not the person that I needed to converse with. The person that should have been honest was my husband who allowed another woman to do his dirty work and so I washed my hands of my confession as well as Trent's betrayal. What I had been begging to know had finally come to the light. All of the lashing out, secret meetings, late nights, perfume odor had a root. Thanks to Trent, my night led to an unexpected detour.

With no thoughts on what I hoped to gain from this visit, I responded to Tim and prepared myself with the most blurred vision and broken heart for I was now thinking with emotion only. Loyalty was obviously not valued by my husband when dealing with our marriage and if he was going to carry on with another woman in an actual relationship, why should I beat myself over the head on account of an innocent kiss?

All Tim wanted to do was talk and I saw no harm in doing so.

CHAPTER TWELVE

More Than A Talk

I remained parked outside, looking at Tim's shop and bracing myself to walk in the front entrance and hear what he had to say. Part of me wanted to turn around and head back home until I spoke with Trent, but the other part wanted to stay and clarify the issues that had now been created at the hands of an intimate kiss.

Not wanting any employees to see me enter into the building so late at night, I sent a quick text asking Tim if all personnel had gone home for the evening before exposing my presence. He responded in seconds assuring me that he was surrounded by cars and office work only and that he would meet me around back as the front door was locked for security purposes.

Sitting for a few more moments as I did not want to look anxious coming in so fast, I exited the driver side door of my car in route of an unknown path. While walking towards the back, a thousand and one thoughts ran through my mind of how I envisioned this conversation. The one thing I knew for certain was that Tim needed to be the one to apologize. He knew that I was married as I made it clear and still crossed a boundary that was not respectful. I only hoped at this point with enough time to think, that Tim would own his wrong doing and be man enough to look me in my face and genuinely apologize, otherwise, our future business with one another would be non-existent and I would have to find myself a new mechanic to service my car.

Just as I turned right towards the back of the building, I was greeted by both Tim who obviously had been waiting outside a short time along with a startling vibration of my phone which I had placed in my back pocket. Unable to greet Tim verbally, answering my phone, I could not yet give my undivided attention which he did not appear to mind as he held the back door open for me before entering and securing it himself.

"Hello!" A frantic Stacy was on the phone and as much as I had enabled her to reach out to me when in need and would usually drop what I was doing to listen, I had my own agenda tonight and simply could not focus on anything else, especially knowing that her daily news was nothing that could not wait until the following day.

Before cutting the call short, I respectfully allowed her the floor to at least paint a picture of her situation before letting her know that we would have to discuss the specifics tomorrow.

"Lesley, this is the third night this week that my husband has not come home. I've called him with the phone going straight to voicemail. I've texted him with no response and I have even reached out to his friends who cover up for him, telling me that they don't know where he is. What do I do?"

What you do is put your foot down and stop allowing him to take advantage of you coming and going as he pleases, but as always, I made certain that my thoughts did not become verbal. Stacy had created this monster and now she was paying the price for being so accepting of his wrongdoings. This certainly was not a conversation that I felt like having tonight for I was in the presence of Tim and he and I had unfinished business to attend to.

I whispered over to Tim who had been patiently waiting at the back exit door along with myself as I remained in a stand still position, listening to Stacy's nonsense. Holding my palm over the speaker of the phone while following him to his office,

I apologized for being rude and quickly wrapped up the conversation. With a half-smile and head nod, Tim appeared understanding of my need to answer the phone.

Had tonight's crisis been any different, I would have probably remained on the phone, but seeing as though it involved the same person committing the same act towards the same individual, our conversation would have to reconvene in the morning. Now to get her to stop talking long enough to interrupt her rant would be the next challenge.

I waited for the perfect moment as she attempted to catch her breath to place this conversation on hold and although the wait seemed forever, it finally came, "Hey T?" She just kept babbling as if she did not even know her own name even after stating it three times which is why I went up in tone. "T! I will call you first thing in the morning ok. I have something really important that I have to take care of right now."

It was funny that no matter what I went through and although I did not open up much, I would at least let Stacy know when life was getting to me and never was she one to lend a shoulder. She was the type of friend whose problems came first, second, and last leaving no room for anyone else's.

When signaling that I was preparing to get off of the phone, Stacy always had to throw in some form of guilt, wishing that her marriage was like mine as if she were depositing an extra quarter in a payphone searching for more time or extra sympathy, "You and Trent probably have something romantic planned and here I am alone bothering you. You go ahead and go Lesley. I'm sorry for interrupting you two."

It drove me nuts how many people assumed that my marriage was perfect at the sight of a smile on my face including Stacy. If only she knew that I was not actually with Trent this evening and that like her husband, my husband wasn't coming home either. Instead of leaking that information, I used her final words as closure to our conversation and said, "Good night lady. Keep your head up."

Ending the call with my hand on my forehead, I took a deep breath and looked at Tim with frustration painted on my face, biting down on my bottom lip. It was bad enough that I had problems at home to battle, issues to discuss with Tim, now I was adding Stacy's debacle to the triangle. I felt like I just could not escape life's madness. I was ending one drama filled conversation only to walk head first into another.

As rude as I felt that I had been, attempting to end a call

which took well over ten minutes, I felt the need to apologize again before getting to the reason for the meeting, "I'm sorry. A friend of mine is going through a lot with her husband right now and she needed me."

Responding not a single word, Tim stared at me as if he were waiting for me to open up the lines of communication while I looked back at him waiting on the same.

While searching for some type of verbal contact, I glanced over in the very corner that Tim kissed me in and began to replay the moment in mind until my daydream was interrupted as Tim's phone began to rattle on his office desk.

It was now time for me to return the very respect that had been given, allowing Tim to converse with the party on the other end of the phone which I was accepting. Instead he looked at the screen, grunted, and threw it back on the desk with a look of disgust. Clearly whoever was on the other end was not at all important and took Tim to a place that forced me to step in and speak as he became agitated.

"Is something wrong Tim?"

Grabbing his phone again as it was now giving off repetitive musical chirps, I could not help, but wonder if a female may be the cause of his mood change and if I should even be in his presence any longer. The more that I thought about it, Tim had spent so much time worrying about my life that not once had I asked or he willingly disclosed his personal life to me. Having been in both his car and office, there was no indication of any female he may be involved with, but that meant absolutely nothing, especially coming from a man. Because I felt uneasy, I decided to wrap things up, no longer wanting to speak. "Tim, I think I better go."

Grabbing my phone from his desk, he placed his palm over my hand and asked me to stay which triggered flashbacks from earlier in the day.

Not wanting to cross this path again, I jerked my hand back quickly and stood from my seat, making my way to the door.

Almost to the finish line as the exit was in plain sight, I was stopped by Tim's voice. He had to be less than a foot away from me as I could hear his words vibrate off of my neck causing the tiny hairs on my skin to rise, "Lesley please don't go."

Not certain as to how close he actually was, I turned

around as slow as possible and asked Tim what else he needed from me because the vibe that I felt in the office told me to get out of the building all together, "Is there something you need to say because obviously you have other business to attend to?"

Unable to answer my question, Tim looked at me like the cat captured his tongue when confronting the nonstop phone calls. His silence made me realize that I had no idea whether or not Tim was married, separated, engaged, in a relationship, situation, or single for that matter. I had no business in this shop after hours and could not stay another second which is why I picked my feet up and continued walking despite his plea to remain.

Reaching out for my hand as it assisted my guidance towards the other side of the door, Tim used just enough force to stop me and pleaded one final time, "Lesley. I beg you don't go."

Other than an apology I had yet to receive, what was so important that he had to keep me near?

I turned around for the second and hopefully final time as we were now a few feet apart and walked directly in front of him, focusing in on his eyes as I asked one very important question which would determine whether or not I entertained any further conversation, "Who do you continue avoiding on your phone?"

This was a very important question because I was not in the business of keeping another woman's man company. If he thought he was going to get away with a lie, he was sadly mistaken. I had had enough practice with Stacy's husband to learn the tricks of a deceitful man.

With his hand outstretched towards his office, Tim asked, "Would you come back into my office and I will explain?"

Looking at the time on my phone, I entertained his request, setting a timer as I only wanted to remain fifteen more minutes.

Seeing Tim attempt to close the door, I requested that it remain open. There was no need to be confined and as I stated to myself with one minute already lost, I would remain only fourteen more minutes.

Watching him fill his cheeks with air on both sides, I could tell that Tim was a bit nervous to share with me whatever it was he was going to and so I waited, forcing nothing on him. It was not my job to prompt the conversation or tell him what I wanted to hear. He had thirteen minutes and whether or not anything came from the current state of silence was up to Tim.

Inhaling and exhaling one final time, Tim began to take me on a journey of his past which would become the first bit of history I would learn of this mysterious man, "I used to date the woman that continues to call me. Actually, I was madly in love with her."

From Tim's somber facial expression along with the past tense choice of words stating that he ONCE loved this woman, I could tell that this relationship did not have a happy ending.

"We met in high school and things moved pretty fast for us. No matter how many times my parents advised me not to get serious, I couldn't help myself. I loved her so much that I asked her to marry me."

Once the word marriage rolled off of his tongue, my body instantly consumed itself with anxiety. Had anyone stood before me, you could actually see my heart beating out of my chest. I feared that he was about to tell me he was married and the thought that I had partaken in an intimate moment with another woman's husband was no easy pill to swallow. Trying not to draw any conclusions, I remained halfway in my seat trying not to let my anxiety show. Depending on the remainder of the story, I was prepared to hit the door, never to return.

With my eyes hanging out of each socket and my hand motioning for him to continue the conversation he had paused, gawking at the phone that continued to vibrate, Tim pressed on, but made no further eye contact as if he were about to confess, "A month before the wedding I caught her in bed with another man and it crushed my soul. Here I was working my ass off to provide for her and our future family asking nothing of her and she was sleeping with a friend of mine that I was going to go in business with."

From the outside, you would never know that any of this had happened to Tim. He wore a glow and had such an inviting character. Listening to his story forced me to no longer question why he needed me to remain in his shop for I could tell that he needed to release such hurt.

I had stayed so long wanting to know more of the story that I had forgotten that I placed myself on a time restriction. All I could do was shake my head in disbelief that someone would hurt such a gentle soul.

While shaking my head, I could see a tear in the corner of his left eye, one in which he tried very hard to hide, "We still talk from time to time which I'm now regretting opening that door. I've been keeping my distance, second guessing any further conversation and as you can see, she continues to blow my phone up."

I had to say, it was a sigh of relief learning that he was not married after all. I was glad that I stayed for had I not, I would have vanished on account of an assumption.

The one thing about me which I took pride in was the fact that I had a lot of empathy. Whenever someone entrusted me with personal information, I could actually place myself in their shoes and gain an understanding of their hurt. Tonight, I had entered Tim's soul learning that the person he once loved hurt him which bonded us as Trent was now involved with another. The pain was real and I could totally sympathize.

I wanted to tread lightly on both my reaction and response for I had yet to give either because I was not sure how fragile his heart was or how recent the cheating had occurred, "I'm sorry that happened to you Tim. If you don't mind me asking, what made you decide to speak with her again? I mean that must have taken a lot of courage."

Tim had now become the mirror image of myself. Although I had not physically caught Trent in bed with another woman, it was clear from his late nights, stays away from home, distance, attitude, and now Traci, he was cheating. I guess I needed to know how one would move forward in that position and with Tim holding such a positive attitude in sight of others, I just had to know how to move forward with or without Trent in my life.

His appearance, when asking him questions, was puzzling as if he did not have a logical response to offer, but he did attempt to gather his words the best that he could and I took notes, "I guess I just wanted to see if there was anything left. Seeing her again did allow painful memories to resurface, but it also reminded me of some of our happiest moments together. Things started off great in the beginning and I thought that I could forget the past, but the more I was around her, the more the happy memories faded away and the bad ones clouded over me. I just hope that she gets the hint and just moves on."

The fact that this woman continued to call Tim numerous times, one could only hope that she was not crazy enough to stop by while I was still in the building and develop the wrong idea. I wanted no part in anyone's unfinished business and from the sound of it, even though Tim expressed to me that he was maintaining his distance, he had yet to tell her which is probably why she was still pursuing what she wanted and thought that the feeling was mutual.

As much as he had been a support to me, I was going to shed some light on him about women and where he was going wrong which was actually a new leaf for me. I was used to listening for offering advice often swayed people to react in a manner based on my opinion and their emotions, but Tim was different and I thought he may find my words insightful as we had developed a friendship.

While Tim sat, trapped in a daze, I stood, walking around the room with plans to leave after my advice, "The reason that she is acting in this manner is because you have yet to tell her how you truly feel from the sound of it. If it is really over between the two of you then you owe it to her to be honest. If a part of you still feels something and has uncertainties about the future, then maybe you both need to sit down and discuss moving forward. You can't just ignore her without giving any clarity. That isn't right. No matter what she did in the past, you don't hurt someone just because they hurt you."

Looking over my shoulder, I could tell that I was getting

somewhere with Tim as he continued to nod throughout my speech and hoped that he would take my friendly advice to heart. Now I did not know this woman, but what I did know was that until Tim spoke up or she got tired of playing cat and mouse, this game between them would continue until someone got hurt all over again.

No longer worried about what happened between the two of us today after learning new details of Tim's past, I felt this a great opportunity to leave him in his office to think about his next move with his ex. I walked over from the corner I had positioned myself and in a friendly manner, rubbed the back of a man whose mood had gone from energetic and sweet, to distant and cold just as I prepared to depart, "Keep your head up Tim." I turned around before walking out of the already opened door and repeated a very important bit of advice as a good friend would, "Talk to her."

As if the office door had been suctioned closed, in front of me was no longer an opportunity to freely walk out which caused me to turn around. Yet again, Tim was right behind me just standing with a blank stare along with an arm stretched out completely, indicating that he was the reason for the door closing.

Caught off guard, I made sure that he and I did not have any unfinished business from the impromptu events of the afternoon, "Tim?"

I gently shook Tim to defrost him from his frozen position and out of nowhere he grabbed both of my arms that I used to grasp his attention, placed them around his neck while using my bottom, as leverage to lift my entire body off of the ground, drawing me over to his desk.

It was in his chair where he planted both of our bodies and began to gently suck on my neck. My mind caused me to pull back only once, and after that moment Tim was like a magician who had hypnotized my entire state, causing me to let go and let Tim.

From top to bottom, my back was being massaged by his masculine hands while my lips were being caressed. The next thing I knew, we were both shirtless, my hands examining his chest and my tongue following in action. He was so fit and I could not help, but express my amazement in my own romantic fashion. Obviously hitting a sexual peak, Tim lifted me up from the chair and carefully laid my body back on his desk. He used his hand to rub all the way down my body, lifting back up to remove my bra. He then introduced himself to each nipple, sucking them one at a time, forcing a quick rise of excitement while my hands gently stroked the back of his head. This intimate bond continued for all of five minutes before the night took off for the both of us.

While my body remained pleasured by this man I had originally come to set straight this evening, the next thing I heard was the zipper of my denim jeans heading in a downward position, my pants lowering past my thighs. After this, nothing, but stillness which intrigued my sense of sight.

This pause that transpired brought me back to life for a moment and I knew that I had gone overboard. Before anything else happened, at this moment, I had the power to stop right here and right now.

Breathing heavily as I was aroused, I utilized the tiny bit of self-control that I had left and reached out to gain his attention, "Tim."

Assuming that my calling out to him was an indicator of my enjoyment, he continued. He remained in his seat with both hands wrapped around my thighs, his eyes glued to the opening of my vaginal area, hidden underneath a purple lace thong.

Holding on to his hands, wrapped firmly around my

thighs, my thoughts voiced a decision that I wasn't sure my body agreed with, "Tim, I think I should go."

Finally, he responded as I lifted my back with both elbows holding my balance on the desk, "Lesley, you are so beautiful Baby."

I could not recall the last time that Trent called me beautiful. I was in such awe from this statement given by Tim that I did not know how to feel or what to do until he requested that I lay back. A slight push with his right hand to my stomach, he eased me back comfortably on his desk.

My thong inching away from my side, he began to talk to my clitoris with his tongue, his lips forcing me to moan. Tim had gotten so involved that my entire body began to quiver and as much as I wanted to return the generosity, he showed his dominance by asking me to remain in my position of comfort.

My body was in such a trance that I had no idea he had completely removed my pants until he surprised me, spreading my legs apart, joining me on the desk. His penis had greeted the top of my vagina while, his lips reintroduced themselves to my chest. One thing led to another and I could feel him deep inside my inner wells. This was nothing like sex with Trent which was forceful, full of complaints, and fast. Tim knew just what to do, no direction required.

He made certain that I was comfortable at all times, but did not produce any form of protection and although I was enjoying myself, I could not overlook this important detail.

While he continued going in and out with my legs wrapped tightly around his waist, his head rubbed against the side of my face where I whispered, "We need a condom Tim."

Tim hit a spot that triggered a form of amnesia and made me forget that we were unprotected. The next thing I felt, warm cum entered inside of my body.

As much as I thought that Tim would just rise, pull his pants up, and walk away, he instead rested on my chest where he leaned forward and kissed my forehead with great compassion. It was here that I realized that I too, had just become as deceitful as my husband by cheating and I wasn't sure that I could ever look at myself the same again.

This was not the plan and the person I had just had sex with was not my man.

CHAPTER THIRTEEN

COMMUNICATION LOST

After sleeping with Tim, one could definitely say that things in my life had changed. I had come home that evening filled with guilt and resentment as I had allowed one kiss along with a state of loneliness to bring me to the most intimate act with another man.

To my surprise, upon pulling up to the driveway of our house, I noticed that Trent was actually home for once and the fear of walking in the house was almost unbearable. Not to mention, it was after one in the morning and I knew that I would have some explaining to do.

You see, I was a home body and unless I was leaving for work, going to the grocery store, or out with Trent, one would find me at home. Coming in at this hour, red flags were sure to be set off. I could only hope that my facial expression would contain itself, not giving away the true events of the evening before gathering enough courage to admit myself, what I had done.

With each second I used to stall unlocking the front door, snapshots of questions appeared in my mind that Trent may ask; would he want to know where I was and who was occupying my time? Would he question the scent of an unfamiliar cologne practically covering my entire body? Would he meet me at the door, aroused, with an urge for sex? Would he question the new rhythm in my hips that Tim had brought out of me, making it easier to bend over, a position Trent would always complain that I did not perform properly? These were all questions brought on by a guilty conscience that continued to grow more worrisome. None the less, I had to face the music if asked and explain how one touch and time apart, transitioned into falling for and sleeping with a man he was unfamiliar; one who was only supposed to service my car, not my body.

Turning the knob slowly as I crept into the front door like a teenager out past curfew, I was greeted not by my husband at first; a huge sigh of relief, but with luggage aligned from the living room sofa to the front door. This made me wonder if he had already been made aware of my indiscretion by another party, but who, was the question. Our circles did not intermingle and I could not think for the life of me who would have reported back to my husband the devastating news that was bound to tarnish my reputation as a wife and lead us straight to divorce court.

While staring at the luggage, preparing to respond to his accusations based on the story he had been told, footsteps welcomed themselves into the room. My heart practically stopped, in need of immediate resuscitation for judgement day had been revealed. I braced myself waiting for the yelling to begin just before staring into Trent's eyes. He had yet another bag to add to the collection of luggage and did not once yell, shout or holler which any other time, I would be grateful as this was a daily routine for him, but on a night like tonight, I needed to get a sense of where his head was.

Trent displayed no feelings or anger, and spoke not a single word, focusing on his luggage solely. As much as I knew that these could very well be our final moments together as a married couple, I decided to tread lightly at least until I could get a clear sense of Trent's state; only then would I decide whether or not to let my skeleton out of the closet. For now, I would initiate small talk, "What are all of the bags for Trent?"

Ignoring both questions I had just asked as if I were an invisible ghost, Trent paraded around the house in his own little world and I knew now, based on the exploitation of his demeanor which was starting to somewhat flare, something was on his mind. Not wanting to spark an argument, I said no more and gave him his space. The ball was now in Trent's court and only when he was ready to speak, would we start over in conversation.

Resting on the couch in the living room, wanting not to find myself in Trent's way as he was clearly on a mission, I sat and observed his strut around the house.

By two in the morning, after retrieving items from various rooms in our home as if he wanted to leave nothing behind, Trent sat across from me and outstretched both of his arms. Resting them on the back of the couch opposite of the one I sat, staring, as if he were analyzing all of the places Tim had seductively touched. I counted down the moments before he spoke, hoping that he would remove his eyes as if he were picturing the areas Tim had intimately placed his hands. Out of nowhere, a once silenced Trent, spoke, "I'm going away for a while and no, I don't know when I'm coming back."

He was so calm with his delivery which was almost scary. Was he leaving based on what he knew, but had continued to keep secret? Why hadn't he questioned his wife coming in the house well after hours? What would make a man leave at two in the morning with multiple bags of luggage? The more I thought about it, I began to wonder if this sudden urge to depart to wherever land had anything to do with the infamous Traci that had introduced herself through a shocking text message. I may not have had much room to judge, but I had been through enough with Trent the past couple of months to lead me to this point. I needed him to own up to his actions and come clean so that I may as well. After both of our disclosures, he could either choose to stay and possibly work things out or walk away from this entire marriage. Two wrongs did not make a right, but two secrets, one from each party, only hindered our relationships growth.

If Trent was leaving because somehow, he had found out about me sleeping with Tim, he had yet to state the facts which now made me question if he did know what I had done or if his mind were focused on something completely different. This became the perfect opportunity to revert the tension towards him and bring up Traci which I wasn't sure if he knew that I was aware.

I leaned forward on the couch and allowed my hands, which were in prayer position, to rest on my lap as I asked a very important question directed at my husband, "This sudden

Jasmine Herring's, *More Than Enough*
168

urge to leave in the middle of the night, does it have anything to do with Traci?"

Smiling bright as the sun as if the sound of her name filled his stomach with butterflies, Trent moved from his rested position on the couch, glanced at the screen of his phone, and grabbed his bags. Heading out of the door, Trent failed to respond at the fact that I had mentioned his secret lover.

This time I was not going to chase my husband out of the house for if he left, there would be no reason to search any longer for the truth that lied within him.

As I suspected he would, Trent chose to leave with unanswered questions that he knew I was seeking and therefore, nothing was left to be said. I had put on a charade long enough pretending that I was happy in my marriage, smiling when I really wanted to break down. I was finally going to make Lesley happy. There was no more that I could say or do and the thought of chasing after a man who made it clear that he did not want to be chased, made me look almost desperate even though he was my husband. If I wanted to live and be free, I would have to make that happen for myself and I did.

Tim and I began spending each and every moment that

we could in his office; sometimes enjoying a meal together, often times learning more and more about the other through conversation, but most of the time, sharing a moment of passion whether that be a simple kiss or further intimacy. We had spent so much time together since our first sexual encounter that time apart was unfamiliar to us.

Still wanting to remain discrete, upon each arrival to Tim's office as this was the only place I felt at peace, I chose to enter in through the back of the building which Tim was not happy at first. Out of respect for my comfort level and relationship status as I was still technically married, he went along with my terms of whatever this was that we were honing in on.

This total stranger who had extended himself to me, was now an active participant in my life, one I did not want to let go. Tim had lifted my spirits and brought me to such a high that I ignored the fact that Trent had not once contacted me since leaving in the middle of the night, over a month ago. I had no idea where he was headed and if he had safely arrived to his destination and to be honest, where I was mentally, the answers no longer phased me.

I had spent so many nights crying and pleading with my

very own husband to show me the love he once expressed before we married and my cries were all silenced by his walking out of the door, resolving not a single marital issue we shared. All of the wants and desires I had in which Trent ignored, Tim saw to that they were met.

Each morning I was greeted with heartfelt wake up text messages just to let me know that I was on Tim's mind. In the afternoons, I was invited to lunch at the shop, not once turning down the opportunity to be in his presence. In the evenings, after departing for a short while, I returned with a night of romancing, where Mr. McWilliams played the director and I, the leading lady. With Tim, I felt like a brand-new woman who had been brought from the dead, revived, and was now full of life she never knew existed.

Many would find that my behaviors were inexcusable and that I could have avoided much that had already transpired and though I did not disagree, you could not tell my mind, body, or soul to turn down the high that it had yearned for so long and had finally received.

My feelings for Tim were developing at a fast rate and with Trent gone and Tim fulfilling the emptiness that lied at the core of my soul, what reason did I have not to accept what I deserved?

CHAPTER FOURTEEN

OTHER WOMAN NOT

No longer dwelling on the past, my life was moving forward and I with it. I had recently been nominated by a group of my fellow colleagues, to launch our firms newest campaign which was a complete honor. Due to the work load, I was to select one other member to help assist in the project's success and completion. Despite everyone else's reservations, I chose Stacy as my right hand which many found this decision, a recipe for disaster.

Lately, she had been on the up and up and as always, I was more than willing to go to bat for her and allowed the talents that she possessed to be showcased. Due to her impromptu emotional instability, the staff felt her incapable of seeing the project through, but with a little coaching, I knew that when it came to business and teamwork, Stacy would not let me down.

To further aid in my confidence level, Stacy continued to glow around the building which gave me all the more assurance

Jasmine Herring's, *More Than Enough*

that she was finally getting on track with her life, I had heard nothing about her husband for about as long as mine had been away although Trent did finally decide to return home, but in different form than before his departure.

When I say that Trent was nice, I'm not talking about a bully deciding to give its prey the day off to pick on someone else kind of nice. I mean the type of nice where you complete a purchase at the grocery store, drop a one-hundred-dollar bill from your wallet to the ground unnoticed, and a complete stranger hands it to you without thinking twice about keeping what is not rightfully theirs.

Assuming there was motive behind these random acts, I chose to ignore what was more than likely only going to last a short while before the real Trent showed his ugly form. Not to mention, Trent had failed to hold up his end of the finances while on hiatus from both our home and marriage, leaving me to enter into our house after a long exhausting day of work to find that our lights had been turned off for failure to make a payment. Talk about having no family in town and not wanting to reveal to your coworkers the hidden truths that shaped your marriage, forced me to remain in an empty home where a dark cloud of anger and fury clouded around me.

Now he was home and wanting to make small talk as if he left things in great standing between us and what, I was supposed to be an active listener and participant. No. He could save his words for whoever he was away with because these ears had been conditioned to listen to a certain sweet, melodic, calming voice. The voice of Tim, who had been a bit distant the past week, placing slight worry into my midst.

The text messages that were once daily and uplifting, were now sporadic and very short. Our lunch and dinner dates we shared had died down to once a week if that and not wanting to give the impression that I was clingy, needy, or with too much time on my hands, I accepted this momentary set back in this unknown destination that we were once traveling together now seemingly in opposite directions. I only hoped that Tim was not losing interest because deep within and this was a revelation that I planned to keep bottled inside for eternity, I needed him. He had accustomed me to a certain lifestyle and new routine that was now thrown off track for undisclosed reasons. I was not sure whether to panic or take a deep breath and relax. I mean he was the owner of a very successful automobile shop which he explained in the beginning, kept him pretty occupied so I couldn't be upset that he was working hard.

All I could do was wait and remain as productive and focused elsewhere to minimize the fear that could now be detected on the follicles of my face. I never thought I would see the day where Stacy would prance around the office floating on air while I sat back, battling internal issues, trying not to solicit exposure. For whatever reason, it was much easier to put on a show for my coworkers when problems arose with Trent in our marriage, but when it came to uncertainties with Tim, the problems were hard to hide and distance even harder to swallow.

"Hey Les! I've got some great ideas for the campaign. What do you say we discuss them over lunch around two, my treat?"

Her treat or not, did this HEFFA just plop her behind on my desk? Don't get me wrong, I loved Stacy, but she was the last person that I wanted to have lunch with and not to mention her bubbly, excited demeanor was quite disturbing.

Of course, I wanted to see her behave in an ecstatic manner considering the fact that I had attempted to get her to this place for some time now, but this was not the day for her to turn over a new leaf. All I could think about was Tim and with him heavy on my mind, I felt unfulfilled and wanted nothing to do with anything or anyone outside of this love affair.

Funny, everyone was so worried about Stacy failing to hold up her end of the project and inside I was now panicking on my own behalf. I was now the wreck and owned the fact that my state of mind was lacking. I needed answers from Tim and I needed them now. I just didn't want to be the one to reach out first, but the anticipation as to when I would finally cross his mind was killing me.

How could he have wooed me for so long, made love all this time without the protection of a condom, having not once pulled out which my husband would not dream of neglecting to do, and now I couldn't even get the slightest greeting as if what we shared meant nothing. My mind was going in circles and I had to get to the root of the sudden shift as my heart was now heavily invested. It was bad enough that I had cheated on my husband and had fallen hard for Tim and as much as I now cared for him, I was not going to be naive enough to allow mind games to be played. If he thought that I was going to forget the last couple of months and just walk away, he was sadly mistaken. I wasn't going to forget him and I would be damned if I allowed him to forget me without an exit interview face to face.

I practically had to drag my feet off of the ground to step foot in the restaurant while accompanying Stacy to lunch. All I wished for the entire time was that this meeting would end so that I could rush home in private and reach out to this man I had grown fond of who was now becoming a remnant of debris in a severe thunderstorm that was quickly whisked away. If I had to sit through one more second of Stacy's over the top animated personality, I was going to scream. I honestly heard nothing that she had to say while voicing her ideas; ONE, I had my phone glued to my palm, twiddling my fingers around and TWO, anytime I heard an alert or felt a vibration from my device, I was quick to rise and stare down at my phone only to find that most of the alerts were emails pertaining to work.

The only time that I did actually notice Stacy was while chomping down on her appetizer having forgotten the etiquette of a lady when in public. Attempting to ignore at first, I could hear Stacy utter the same sound for the second time. Focusing in on my phone, I hoped that just one of these alerts was actually Tim and that somehow, I had just overlooked his message. After the third sound which came from across the table in the very location Stacy sat, I looked up extremely annoyed. Stacy looked directly into my eyes as if we were standing nose to nose with one another. Obviously, the animated sounds that stemmed from her vocal cords were directed to me the entire time in an effort to grasp my attention. Leaving me no choice, but to place my scavenger hunt of missed messages to the side, I digressed my current rude behaviors so that Stacy and I could get our meeting on its proper schedule to prepare for our big day.

Just as Stacy fixed her face to mouth the first word which was a millisecond from making its debut out of her mouth, the name Tim read across my phone and boy did my entire aura switch gears. Both knees tucked tightly underneath the table, reflexed so hard that they not only lifted off of the ground, but also caused the water that remained housed in a glass cup to tip over onto the table and topple to the floor. But forget the water, what Tim had to say was much more important and although I had been anticipating his call or text, as I began to unlock my phone to open the message, a state of fear raced through my body.

What was he going to say after all this time? Had he decided to no longer communicate because me being married was too much for him? Had he and his ex-reconciled?

The only thing left to do was face the music, read the message that remained unanswered, and determine after reading, the direction my life and heart was going to take.

With my eyes closed shut, finger on the read button, I counted to five and read what was either going to make me smile or make me cry, "MISS YOU BABY! COME SEE ME."

Placing the phone to my lips as I took in the message once more, although not physically present, I could feel Tim's arms wrapped around me and I could not help, but melt. My facial expression, bright as the sun, my heart moved by the loving words I had so missed and longed for.

The only thing left to do was excuse myself from Stacy who had been extremely patient with me through this debacle of a lunch, which I did feel bad; however, if only she knew that I was on the right track to getting my internal issues in order, I'm sure she would encourage me as I'd encouraged her in the past to go and do what needed to be done.

Purse already in hand, I stood from the table and faced Stacy before exiting stage right. With my hand pressed delicately on my chest to give off a sincere appeal, I cut our lunch meeting short, "Stacy, something has just come up and I have to go. I'll take care of lunch and call you tonight to further our conversation." A conversation that never really made it anywhere is what I thought of while trying to properly exit.

Not sure whether or not she was about to set it off due to my behavior which she would be well within her rights, I stood still and respectfully made eye contact awaiting my sentencing.

Stacy used both hands to scoot the bottom of her seat back, giving her enough room to rise from her chair to stand as well. Was this woman about to hit me? I couldn't yet tell whether or not she was upset and now questioned if we had further problems that needed to be addressed due to the grunt she let out while standing to meet me. With both arms extended out, Stacy wrapped her hands around me causing a flinch. Then she whispered in my ear, "Go get him girl."

Did she know about Tim or was she still under the impression that my smile was about Trent? Should I confide in her and spill the tea or simply let it be? The longer I remained in a stand still position thinking, the longer it took me to get to Tim. Responding to Stacy's command, "I'll tell my man you said hello."

I never said what man I was referring to for Stacy only knew of one so technically I was not lying to her. Maybe one day

I would come clean to a person other than my diary, but first I needed Tim to come clean with me. Sure the words BABY and I MISS YOU buttered me up, but still did not confess the cause of his newly found distance. If he were dealing with someone else, his ex who was the only person I could think of, then I was no longer going to remain in a compromising position. Holding the title of the other woman was not my character and I would relinquish the title completely if this were the direction we were heading.

CHAPTER FIFTEEN

SOMEONE TO LOVE ME

I marched into Timothy's auto shop, adrenalin high and yes, I did say Timothy. No longer was I going to accommodate even the simplest name preference nor anything else for that matter until I got to the bottom of his disappearing act.

As always, he was overseeing the technicians out in the bay and I could not lie, he looked so damn fine. So fine that I wanted to jump right into his arms, call him daddy while letting him bend me over and spank me. It was something about a hardworking, dedicated man that turned me on, but I had to stop fantasizing, come back down to reality, and remind myself of today's visit for it was not a friendly gathering.

Motioning for me to head to the back, I could see Timothy's eyes begin to droop as we made contact with one another. His lips begin to poke out as if he knew he was about to walk the hall of shame. Keeping my mind focused, I continued to recite in my head a brief pep talk to pump myself up; He was wrong. He better explain. Allow no pitiful facial structure to sway your feelings as you were the one made to worry while in his absence.

Just as we both planted ourselves in the normal seating positions in Timothy's office, my phone began to buzz and what do you know, it was Trent. Wanting nothing to do with him, I was honored to press the ignore button and did with grace, reporting back to the regular scheduled program, Eyes of Lies starring yours truly, Timothy McWilliams. Timothy's pupils were watching and caught me completely off guard as they began to flood with tears out of nowhere, his lips of no word choice.

A demeanor never seen before, I was not sure how to approach a conversation or who should start, causing a stare off battle between his eyes and mine. This game we were playing lasted all of three minutes before an alert came from my phone that I had tucked away in my purses inner pocket.

Failing to grasp the hint as I ignored his call, Trent was now texting me as if I would respond in this form instead. He had nothing for me and I was giving no more energy into a dead relationship killed by a man with the only qualification of a husband, being the wedding band he seldom wore. If my absence from our home wasn't enough, the lack of meal preparation in our kitchen, the complete halt of any and all sexual activity, and not even the slightest of hello's and goodbyes, surely, he had to get the hint by now, but I guess not as he was now questioning my whereabouts. I wanted to respond, "none of your damn business," considering that he never worried about me before, but as that was not my character, I simply asked why and returned back to Timothy who had now positioned his leather office chair towards the window where he could no longer be seen.

I had literally had enough with the mood changes of these men today and could not wait to get to the comfort of my own home, work on my upcoming campaign, and chat with Miss. Diary herself who never seemed to let me down.

As much as I wanted Timothy to be the one to lead the conversation, I was now at peace having accomplished nothing as of yet and could walk away from this office, never to return or look back for that matter. The time was fun, it had filled its purpose and now, I was ready to bury it all in the past.

"Timothy?" Just as I stated his name, he turned, shockingly aware that he was back to Timothy as opposed to Tim, tears trailing down each cheek.

In all my time with him, Timothy was always a burst of energy with a vibrant smile. He was the man that helped you find purpose in life and now, I found myself in the position of putting my feelings to the side to be the friend to him that he had been to me, but of course there had to be further interference. It was Trent, again, texting my phone.

"Do you need to take care of something," asked Timothy. Before responding, I could not help, but stare into his eyes and curiously wonder what was hurting this man inside.

What made this visit confusing was the fact that I had come prepared to lash out at his treatment towards me and here he was, reminding me why I had fallen for him with his concern. Who could stay mad at a person who always placed you first in his life?

I glanced at my phone a final time and it was bugaboo Trent, asking if I had plans for dinner. Yet again with the small talk which I did not care for not because I was currently in the presence of Timothy, but because Trent was showing a different side that was temporary. I was not going to conform to this new-found person for if I did, I would be setting myself up to be hurt when all hell returned back to normal.

Wanting not to stoop to his past level of anger, attitude, and uncompromising ways, I responded with a final message stating, "I'm in a meeting. I do not know what's for dinner or what time I will be home, but you are more than welcome to grab yourself something. I will be fine." Since he always wanted to know when I was coming home so that he would not have to wait on dinner, there was my response. What he did with it, I did not care and proved that by turning off my phone to give complete attention to Timothy who had been more than patient with me.

Treading lightly with my words, uncertain of the depth of his emotional being, I laid it smoothly on the table, allowing my heart to recite what only my diary was made aware, "You know, when I met you, I had no intentions of becoming anything more than a client in your shop. You initiated everything that transpired between the two of us and out of the blue, you become a ghost."

No longer shedding any tears, I was starting to question if Timothy's spur of the moment emotional effects were to keep me in his good grace. Now I was mad as hell and felt taken advantage of, giving me no more motive to filter my words. "From our many conversations, you already knew how fragile my heart was and here I am remaining as far away from you as possible while you continue coming closer and closer to my heart, making it hard to avoid."

I could feel my body temperature rise to a feverish state and with the assistance of an imaginary presence in the room that lifted me up out of my seat and led me to Timothy's desk, I positioned my hands to rest while leaning forward to check him, "I don't make it a habit of sleeping with other men, but with you, all bets were off. You know, for once in my life I felt needed and wanted without having to beg or give much energy for that matter." No longer resting in a still position, I began to walk around Timothy's office, shaking with emotions. "You opened my eyes to a new world and in an instant, at your convenience alone, took everything I had yearned for away. I'm disgusted by my actions and even more upset that I let you get the best of me."

Unable to fight back the tears, I exposed them completely, replaying the last couple of months, wondering what my parents thought up in heaven. This was not the daughter that they raised nor were my actions a reflection of their love and devotion towards one another. Ashamed could not even begin to describe what I felt inside, but THROUGH would define this moment. I had allowed myself to become so vulnerable that I lost sight of all morals and values.

Before I left, I had to exit with a final bow. I mean I wanted him to forever remember my name and not just the action of fornicating with a married woman for he was probably chuckling inside, feeling himself about finally hitting it as little boys would say. Wearing my grown woman hat, I had decided not to yell, scream, or reiterate our time shared, but to release my hands from his desk, stand mighty and proud for the reality of it all was the fact that I could not take back any actions of mine that led to this day. I placed my thumb and index finger underneath his chin, leaned to his level just enough to gaze into his eyes, pressed my lips against his left earlobe, and whispered, "The next woman you do this too may not be as subtle as myself."

I said this because if I were in fact the first woman he had hit and quit, playing the disappearing act, resurfacing as he pleased, he needed to know that others may not be as passive as I had been. This was the best advice that I could give.

I made the adult decision to ask questions first before reacting even though I felt used. Other women may very well act first and ask questions later. This made me think of his ex, whom he had yet to gain courage to confront and express that he was through. At some point, he was going to meet his match and I prayed it would not end poorly for him.

Jasmine Herring's, *More Than Enough*

As I began to remove my face from his ear, he whispered into mine, "I LOVE YOU!" Lifting up with the assistance of Timothy's chest, using both of my hands to push him back, causing his seat to roll, I was not going to sit and play mind games.

Did this man just state that he loved me? He must have thought that I was an idiot. I was not buying his words for they were stated in false pretense. Had this very statement been true, why distance yourself? Had this been true, why not just come out and say it the second we closed the door to the office? I gathered the feeling that he was only stating the three words every woman wants to hear because he was losing his pleasure, which is probably what he thought of me and I was not giving in. In fact, I made the executive decision to walk out of the door.

"Lesley hear me out Baby." This man grabbed onto my lower legs as he planted his knees on the ground while holding me hostage near his desk leaving me no choice, but to remain and listen.

His eyes began to water up again which placed my body in a still trance, ears wide open while Timothy made his peace, "The reason that I have been distant with you is because I was trying to fight my feelings for you. You know that I have been hurt before and the last thing I wanted was to be hurt again."

I'm trying to figure out while he is pleading with me just why he thought that I would hurt him. Had I done so yet? I had given myself completely to this man no matter how hard I tried to fight it. He was more than half of my diary and I had no problem sharing all the outs and ends of my life with him.

At this moment the gears shifted between Tim and I and yes, he was back to Tim. I had a confession to make as well, but not before asking a very important question. While Tim remained glued to the ground, still holding on to me, occasionally rubbing against my thighs and resting his face, I altered the direction of his head so that I could look into his eyes while asking, "Are you and her back together?"

A person's eyes are said to be the voice of one's soul and I needed him to be honest before I allowed my heart to invest any further.

Using my waist as a crutch to stand, Tim held on to my face and responded, "I love you and I only want to be with you. There is nowhere else I'd rather be."

Although not completely satisfied with the response to my question, I wanted to be loved so much that I accepted his omission as fact. This moment, right here and right now, I declared that Tim was the man for me. My marriage was over without the legal formality and a new beginning was presenting itself and I could not be more excited to enjoy the ride. Tim had shown me time and time again that I mattered and if it was not made clear any other day, today I knew that he was mine and I was his.

The emotion and affection we shared filled the entire office space. One might as well place a DO NOT DISTURB sign on the outside door because boy did we go at it so much so that I too verbalized my inner soul in the heat of passion, "I LOVE YOU TOO!"

I had finally found the peace that I had searched for, the love I had longed for, and the man I had hoped for. He was mine and I was his and that was the way it was going to stay.

CHAPTER SIXTEEN

REPLACEMENT

Confined to the bed this morning, I was battling a stomach bug that didn't seem to want to remove its grip from my body. Although I felt like death and wanted to remain nestled in my bed, the campaign was two weeks away and temporary illness was no excuse not to be fully prepared.

Pulling energy from where ever I could, I forced my body to sit in an upright position in an effort to slowly get my day started. Standing obviously way too fast, on my toes less than three seconds, I found myself running to the restroom where the next visual I had was that of the bottom of the toilet.

Slouched forward, using the toilet as a headrest, I raised my neck up while holding my hair back, puzzled as to the route of this out of the blue spell. I could not recall eating anything out of the ordinary and although a bit stressed lately, my body was used to the demands of my life and had never failed me before.

Thank goodness that I did not have to meet Stacy until noon which would allow my body time to move at its own pace without the sense of urgency.

Having completed a rough copy of our speech, Stacy and I had to work the ends and odds out to perfect what was sure to be a winning campaign. To no surprise at all, she had been the real MVP with this project she was co-directing, alongside myself. I mean I did not have to ask for anything and our meeting of the minds was on one accord, making this project flow to perfection. Now if I could just find my briefcase and make it out of the door without having to detour to the downstairs bathroom, that would be my first accomplishment of the morning.

Step by step, I walked slowly down the stairs, stomach turning left and right. As usual, I could smell the aroma of coffee that Trent made a routine ritual, brewing each and every morning. Having no reason whatsoever to join him in the kitchen for I had ceased any attempts of morning conversation for some time now, I searched elsewhere for my briefcase and found it resting on the side of our living room coffee table.

Feeling slightly faint while bending down to reach for my briefcase, I grabbed on to the arm rest of our couch while allowing the cushion to catch my fall in plain sight of Trent, who was exiting the kitchen. Unlike ever before, he rushed to my aid and asked, "Are you ok," with the sound of true concern.

Unfortunately, I was not moved by his charismatic behavior in my time of crisis and shrugged his hand off of my shoulder as he had begun to rub while I was slouched forward, holding my stomach with one hand, covering my mouth with the other, to catch what I knew was stirring up inside. Attempting to console me again using his sense of touch, I turned in the direction of Trent to remove his hand for the second time, in a stern voice stating, "I'm fine Trent. You can go and do whatever it is you were preparing to do."

Had he forgotten the introduction of Traci? Had he forgotten the countless nights I begged for his love and affection, going to sleep alone in a bed made for two? Had he forgotten the fact that I would have never ever met Tim who was slowly, but surely taking Trent's place right underneath his nose had he been man enough to take my car into the shop himself? Had he forgotten how his negligence left me alone in the dark with no lights in our home or even given me the heads up that he had not paid the bill? Thanks to Trent, I was made to believe that my birthday was just another day and not even worth the crack of a smile nor joy inside. Why would I welcome anything that he had to offer at this point?

Traci could have all that Trent had held back from me for so long now including these little phony back rubs which did the opposite of improving my state, instead irritated the hell out of me.

Needing to greet Stacy for our meeting slash lunch and no longer wanting to be in the presence of Trent for I was becoming upset, I began to make my way to the door where he followed like a trained dog to his master, assisting me as if I had a severe ailment.

Playing *ring around the rosie*, I continued to circle around my car as Trent followed, first placing my briefcase in the backseat.

Making it to the seat of the driver side, Trent grabbed hold of the door where he almost lost a hand, knelt down, and asked the most shocking question of all, "May I join you at church this Sunday?"

Eyes squinted together, nose turned up, I sat and stared, processing Trent's request. Anyone else would have been welcoming to a person wanting to attend church to get close to the Lord, but with Trent oh was the story a bit different.

Having asked Trent to tag along every Sunday for the past four months, this question asked out of love and wanting him by my side in the church pew, caused numerous altercations in our home. Sometimes he got so frustrated that he would begin to yell and ridicule me for even participating in what he called, a money hungry church. He hated that I sat and listened to a person dictate to me for two plus hours and despised the fact that I gave my offering for he felt it was being deposited right into the pocket of the pastor himself. Now all of a sudden, he wanted to go to the one place he had a strong stance against, why?

Curious as to what would even make him bring this topic up, I asked with slight attitude as he had never accepted my invitation before, "You're joking right?" He had to have bumped his head and forgotten the countless arguments that stemmed from the word CHURCH alone.

Laying his hand on mine causing me to pull it back, resting it on the center console, Trent held his head high, looked at me with a gaze of seriousness, took a deep breath and answered, "I just think that it's time for me to get right with God and correct many errors that I have made in the past."

Was he referring to the cheating, mistreatment, neglect

of his wife, time spent away from home, lack of support as a husband? I mean I could go on and write a book about his so-called errors.

Face still frozen with a blank stare, I could not help, but to call his act a bluff. This was not the Trent that I knew and I was not sure what had gotten in to him, but I was so familiar with the Trent a few weeks back that I did not know how to welcome any other. This new, unpredictable Trent was hard to digest.

I would never deny a person the entrance to church and although I knew that Trent was not serious about attending, I played along with his inquiry, knowing in my head, he was not going to show and as always I would be entering into Christ Temple, party of one.

Letting out a deep breath for I knew what response the Lord would have wanted to roll off of my tongue, "Yes Trent. You can come with me to church."

Like a jack in the box at the last turn, Trent sprung up from his knelt position, balled his fists up and yanked his arms back in excitement screaming, "YES," for all of our neighbors to see. I now knew that this man had to be under some form of influence. To go from despising church one minute to being overly excited the next, he was either truly on something or had a come to Jesus moment.

Finally, able to reverse out of the drive way as Trent was now on our front porch away from the car, I could hear him shout from my sunroof, "I'll go pick out my clothes now Lesley."

I called it. He was on crack. Church wasn't for another four days and here he was, jumping up and down on the front lawn like a child who had ingested entirely way too much candy.

If this was Trent's attempt to ease back into my life a better man than before, he need not waste any more time. I had no more energy left to give. My tear ducks had since dried up and my heart no longer recognized the love my husband had shown so long ago.

Trent had been replaced. In my eye, Trent handed me over to the next applicant where I wanted my time forever spent.

CHAPTER SEVENTEEN

SURPRISE

Staring up at the bright light, one would have concluded that I had died and gone to heaven. I would have thought this myself had it not been for the loud monitor going off in my ear along with the painfully irritating iv that my arm was currently bound to.

After returning from the restroom, which was located inside the small cafe Stacy chose to meet for our project update, my body finally gave out. It let me know just how tired it was by knocking me to the ground, no energy to even lift my head from the hardwood flooring. The next thing I knew, having received a mild concussion as a result of the fall, we were in the back of an ambulance which whisked me away to the nearest hospital.

Having come to, I honestly saw no point seeking medical attention, but upon request of the restaurant owner, who was extremely apologetic and wanting to make sure that I was fine or better yet, make certain that they were not liable for negligence in case they were to blame for the incident, I agreed to be checked out. Now we patiently waited the doctor's arrival and by we, I meant Stacy, who after all this time, was finally the friend to me that I had always been to her.

Slightly woozy from the concussion, I did not say much while lying down in the bed, but did want to extend my gratitude to Stacy who was ten days strong, having not uttered one breath about her husband. If you could see the glow on this woman's face with her previous appearance the complete opposite, you would have thought she had found her very own Tim because her expression was the same way I felt every time I even thought his name.

Hand over my eyes as the lighting in the room created more of a headache, I turned in Stacy's direction to verbalize my appreciation, "Thank you for sticking with me!"

She could have gone straight home once emergency personnel arrived, but instead, remained by my side which is more than I could ever say about Trent. Had I called Tim which I did contemplate, I'm sure he would have come as he was known for being my superman, but for this occasion, Stacy was the perfect filler for the job at hand.

With an angelic smile on her face, Stacy gave response to my gratitude, "You know I couldn't leave my girl hanging."

Actually, I didn't considering this was the first time I could truly count, but not wanting to argue or take away the fact that she was here now, I simply accepted her presence for what it was and remained idle, awaiting to be released from the ER.

Wondering what Tim was doing at this time, I really wanted to call him just to hear his voice, but did not want to give even the slightest indication that I was talking to a man that was not my husband. Although Tim wanted to come out to the public displaying me on his arm, he was surprisingly understanding that ONE, my marriage was extremely complicated, but not to the point of divorce as of yet and TWO, that I only felt comfortable behind closed doors in his office; not yet ready to walk on the red carpet with him by my side.

Leading up to this day, Tim had been very patient with our secret relationship. He had not pressured me once which is why I loved him even more and began pondering whether or not I would just go ahead with the divorce. Trent had checked out of our marriage and into a completely new relationship, still not man enough to come out and say it where I myself, remained all cried out finding love elsewhere.

Sitting here daydreaming so long, I almost forgot that Stacy was sitting in the very room that I occupied. From the looks, she didn't seem to notice my daydreaming as she herself was occupied with her cellphone that appeared quite entertaining. She began to bite down on the nail of her index finger with her legs crossed, quietly laughing to herself as though something was arousing her which I could not see.

Inquiring minds were curious and it did not seem that she was going to break the news anytime soon as she kept the phone and her thoughts all to herself. Bored out of my mind, unable to exit out of the four walls of this room, I could do nothing, but pry, "Oh Stacy!"

Mesmerized by her phone, Stacy did not even budge at the sound of her name forcing me to shout, "STACY?"

Hearing me now along with all of the other patients in the rooms nearby, Stacy jumped up, phone falling to her lap almost landing to the ground, and responded frantic as her phone falling was a tragedy, "Oh, I'm sorry Lesley. What's up?"

What's up? That's exactly what I wanted her to tell me. "This vibrancy you've been carrying lately; what's that all about?"

Smiling again while using both hands to rub up and down her thighs, Stacy began to breath heavily and at first, I questioned whether or not I should page the nurse, but watching closely, the breathing began to slow down and the words soon followed, "I'm just in a better place lately that's all. Nothing more, nothing less"

If that wasn't a broad response I don't know what you would call it. I wanted more and she was giving me exactly what she said, less. She was in a different space, but that was not what I asked. I wanted the juicy details. I had heard so much bad that I finally had front row tickets to the good, which she did not want to reveal, unsure why.

In hopes of a different response, I reworded my verbiage, "I can tell that you are in a better place. What do we owe the pleasure?"

Energy resurfacing, I was able to sit up on the side of the bed, allowing my legs, which were covered by a hospital gown, to sway left and right as I leaned in, prepared to learn the mystery behind Stacy. Just as her mouth opened wide, she inhaled, exhaled, and with a slight smirk, left me even more confused, "Wait about three more weeks and I promise I'll tell you everything."

Wait three weeks. What type of news couldn't be revealed for three weeks? Out of all the other devastating news that I was so often made aware of, why did the very news that was bringing her spirits up have to be kept a hidden secret?

Having a go getter mentality and wanting not to wait a second longer, I fixed my lips to ask again, this time hoping that I could persuade Stacy to cut the three weeks short and the moment I asked, in walked the doctor with a clip board in hand, smile on his face.

"Good afternoon! You must be Lesley I presume?"

It would be an even better afternoon once I was released which is exactly what I hoped he was preparing to do.

"Good afternoon doctor!"

Resting in the nearest seat, he rolled it over alongside my hospital bed and began scanning the pages on the clip board coming to a screeching halt, stating two words, "Ah Ha!"

Eyebrows raised, not sure what AH HA meant, I became very antsy as he had yet to give any more than a greeting, something obviously keeping his eyes focused.

Looking back observing that Stacy was in the room, the doctor leaned forward and whispered, "Do you mind if I talk freely or would you prefer that your guest wait outside?"

If I wasn't nervous before, I was now. What did he have to tell me that would make me want to send Stacy out of the room?

A million thoughts began running through my mind and even though I was going to allow her to stay, out of respect and privacy, Stacy excused herself from the room more than likely continuing on with her phone sex with whoever had clearly ended her mighty long sexual drought. Trust me, I knew what that looked like and the girl was practically drooling in need of an ice bath.

Bracing myself for the diagnosis I was about to receive as a result of today's events, lips slightly spread apart, I let out a breath, opened my ears, and awaited news that may determine the rest of my life.

"Lesley, after running standard tests of your blood sample, we detected high levels of HCG."

What in the hell was HCG an acronym for? Hyper, higher, chronic, cancer, gastroid; I could think of a thousand words for each letter, but the more I thought, the higher my blood pressure increased. I needed this doctor to spit it out before I was admitted into the psych ward.

Treading lightly with the question, I nervously asked, "What is HCG?"

Still smiling, he responded, "Human Chorionic Gonadotropin."

This had to be a very, very, very rare disease, one I'd never heard of before and yet the doctor was the only one in the room smiling. I mean come on, a little empathy in my time of mourning would be nice.

Not wanting an exact time stamp as I prepared my next question, I had to know, "How long do I have?"

Busting out in laughter as he obviously had no compassion for his patients, laid his hand on the bed and eased the worry that quickly consumed my body, "Ma'am you are not dying. You're fine with no disease detected."

If I was fine, why the lengthy diagnosis? If I was fine, why didn't he just say that to begin with?

"Lesley, Human Chorionic Gonadotropin is the hormone produced in the body following the embryo implantation. You are pregnant. Based on your HCG levels, I'd say around twelve weeks."

Pregnant?

Unable to speak any longer, I laid back down in the bed in a state of awe where I looked up at the ceiling for comfort.

Pregnant?

I dreamed of having a family and what was supposed to be one of the happiest times in my life, was soon going to become one of the hardest and most challenging.

Tears began to release down each side of my face just thinking of all that was to come of this untimely news.

My life had just become extremely complicated at the hands of both pain and passion. Here I was a married woman, wanting a child with my husband who denied me that right;

now carrying what was beyond a doubt, Tim's child.

The doctor walked out of the room allowing me time to process the news, assuming that my tears were of joy and excitement as he congratulated me. While he was on to the next patient, I remained in the hospital room wanting to be released five minutes prior, now wanting to remain, never walking out of the door.

Getting dressed as slow as possible, I remained in a state of shock with a mental image of my husband in mind. I almost felt bad for Trent as he had been making effort lately to be a better man and although I had lost interest, this news may end any friendship that could result upon conclusion of the divorce I had been leaning towards for some time now. My biggest fear of all, however; was ruining what could be between Tim and I for he was the man that I wanted to be with. Although I knew that he felt the same, I was uncertain how he would feel learning that together, we had created a child.

At almost three months and already showing symptoms, which would explain the morning sickness I thought just a bug along with passing out in the cafe due to my equilibrium being off, both men had to learn what would be devastating to one and life change for the other. As far as who would learn first, I

Jasmine Herring's, *More Than Enough*
209

was not yet sure and how I would come out with it; a mystery in itself.

Walking out of the room with instruction papers to follow up with an OBGYN, I was released and opened the door to face the rest of my life.

Completely forgetting that Stacy was here, I did my best to hide the evidence of my pregnancy, folding the papers in half and hiding it alongside my right leg where she remained positioned on my left.

"What did the doctor say Lesley," asked Stacy as she trailed behind me no longer on her phone.

Unprepared to reveal the news, I continued walking towards the double doors that led to the lobby and almost made it out until I was reintroduced to the doctor who ended the visit with, "Congratulations again!"

Was he serious? Now I knew I was going to have to tell Stacy.

Gently grabbing a hold of my arm, Stacy slowed my stride out of the hospital and looked into my eyes, "Congratulations on what," as she began to poke at my stomach, playing dumb as if she did not know. She was probably standing at the door when the doctor came in and told me; nosey ass.

Anxiety written across my face, I responded with the truth, no longer able to hide, "I'm pregnant."

Here she was jumping up and down in the lobby, the only human in the entire facility appearing happy and enthusiastic while others awaited to be seen or for updates on family members.

Question following even more questions, Stacy just didn't get the hint that this was not yet a joyous occasion for me, but I could not fault her as she had no clue what the last couple of months consisted of for me.

"Do you think your husband is going to be excited?"

Again, I said, she had no clue what the last couple of months had brought to my life especially the fact that my husband, who she thought the perfect man, was not the father and my marriage which she also thought perfect, would soon end learning that I was carrying another man's seed.

Stacy drove me back to the cafe where I remained silent the entire car ride waiting to be reunited with my car left in the parking lot. After popping back in to briefly speak with the owner, who after learning the true reason that lied behind my fall, was ecstatic to say congratulations more so excited that he was not to blame after all and would not be waiting for litigation papers.

Having missed a text from Tim earlier as the reception in the hospital was poor, I decided not to respond through text, but face to face instead. This news was deserving of being in one another's presence for we needed to discuss just how we would move forward whether that be officially together or apart.

Usually I would call ahead or wait for the invitation he extended to come and see him, seeing as though that could be days from now having experienced his disappearance before, I made the adult decision to surprise him and boy was he about to be overly stunned.

CHAPTER EIGHTEEN

SHATTERED

Life as I knew it would never be the same since learning that I was now expecting a child and going to be a mother.

With every stop light I neared, I contemplated turning around, refraining from telling two influential men in my life; my soon to be ex-husband Trent as well as the father of my unborn son or daughter, Tim. The fear was undeniable, but I knew that in order to begin the process of moving forward, I had no choice, but to deal with the outcome of my decisions no matter what they entailed.

After driving in circles around the city, I made the decision to reveal the news to Tim first for more reasons than one. First; he was in fact the father of this baby and as we had created a life together, the decisions we made going forward pertained to the well-being of our unborn. Second; I needed to know his thoughts as to whether or not this baby was going to bring us together, out in the forefront, or drive a wedge

Jasmine Herring's, *More Than Enough*
213

between all we had shared and built. Third; and this was my hope, had he decided to make us a family, I needed to know his plan of action.

My intuition said that Trent, possibly furious once informed, would want to meet the man I was leaving him for and I had to be certain that Tim was on my side and prepared to be the man that I needed and not the little boy who would run and hide. I did not want to face Trent, unknowing of my future even though he was my husband, before introducing the news to the father first. As crazy as it all seemed, I was not for drama or hostile situations and was trying the best that I could to make light of a dark road for all parties involved.

Pulling up to Tim's shop as I had done many times before, this time the visit with a purpose and not sexual endeavors that we had accustomed ourselves to enjoying.

Not yet able to remove myself from my vehicle, I turned the radio on hoping to catch either a powerful message on 1310 or an empowering song that would give me the strength to follow through with what I knew had to be done. Right on time was Maurette Brown Clark's *Sovereign God* and immediately I laid my head back against the driver seat, closed my eyes, and began to pray before delivering my first confession.

Her voice was powerful and words to the song, moving. I honed in on a line as I placed my hand on the inside handle which opened the door to the outside world that I had to face. With every step I replayed her voice in my head, "I will put every situation, into your capable hand, I don't have to know the plan because you are, you are the sovereign God." I did not know God's plan or what position I was going to come out of the shop in, but I knew that he was going to show me a sign which I was prepared to listen and obey.

Holding the pregnancy confirmation in one hand, I opened the entrance door with the other to find that the shop was pretty empty for the time being making this an even better opportunity to gain Tim's full and undivided attention. Hopefully he did not take offense to me coming unannounced and saw this topic important enough to drop whatever he was currently focused on.

Needing not a single escort in the direction of Tim's office as it had become my second home, I walked to the back on a mission to get in and get out. Trailing slow as a snail, I paced back and forth now holding the paper with both hands against my mouth for comfort.

Before me stood a closed door, one in which I was not

sure should remain closed as I was not certain who was on the other side. Wanting not to interrupt, hand shaking, I turned the knob hoping to be as discrete as possible in case Tim were either in a meeting or on an important business call.

Opening the door as slow and as quiet as I could without even a squeak coming from my end, my eyes were in plain sight of Tim. In the very corner we exchanged our first kiss is where I found him and I sure hoped that he had in his mind a happy memory of that day which may make the news a bit more settling to the ear.

Now completely in the room, Tim still facing the corner, I quietly cleared my throat, presence still unknown and as I fixed my lips for a subtle introduction, I noticed Tim reach for his phone that began to ring and instantly, I backed up outside of the door where I left it with only a small crack.

It may have seemed that I was eavesdropping to anyone passing by in the hallway, but I actually gave no thought to his conversation and respectfully waited until he finished to show my face and reveal the news.

Whoever he was talking to on the other end of the phone must have struck a chord because I had never seen Tim appear so angry. He began power walking from one side of the room to the other and with his voice carrying down the hall, must have noticed the office door cracked which he slammed shut with one hand, still unaware that I was there.

Starting to wonder if this was the day I should have this conversation, I began to panic as his appearance was almost scary and his voice, hostile to say the least. Whatever this person was saying to him, I wished that they would hurry up and end the conversation so that I could have my turn hoping he would not respond the way he was currently. This person was not helping my situation at all and one or both of them needed to take a deep breath and reconvene the call at a later date when both were much more calmed down than currently.

Yelling ceased, I assumed that Tim had concluded his call and quietly cracked the door for the second time to find him now sitting in his office chair, resting while looking towards the outside window. Unable to wait any longer, I walked into the office where I heard the chair give off a light sound with Tim sitting up and his voice follow.

He was in fact still on the phone forcing me to wait a moment longer which I did right in front of his desk, this time standing in position until he turned and faced me. I could have easily interrupted, but as if the vibe in the room wasn't already tense enough between his afternoon blow up and my news to add to his day, I went with the flow and unknowingly to him, followed the beat of his drum.

Shifting his tone from high pitched to silent, he seemed to now deliver a slightly more compassionate tone which let me know that he was capable of turning a negative situation into a positive. Right here and right now I knew that there was hope that Tim and I could make what at first may seem like a scary road to travel, a loving outcome to a rocky beginning. This realization also eased the anxiety that had taken over and as soon as he completed his call which from the sound was almost over, I would happily share the news that I now knew he would find joy in as well.

As laughter began to release from the other side of the chair, I could not help, but to find interest in the conversation that at first, I thought business now seemingly personal. So personal that one could now conclude and I would not disagree, I was eavesdropping in on.

"If things are going to work out, I need you to start trusting me more."

To my knowledge, Tim was in business for himself unless there was a mystery co-owner that I had yet to be introduced to. I continued on, missing not a single word.

"I work very hard and you know that. If I'm not coming home, you know exactly where I am. I may have cheated in the past, but you cannot continue bringing my past into our future or this won't work."

What exactly was he stating would not work?

The last I checked and I did very well check, Tim was single and only wanting to be with me. From the sound of things, either he had recently began seeing someone else or had rekindled the relationship with his ex which he told me he was trying to avoid.

Unable to stomach another word and having yet spoken with Tim, I turned my back and proceeded out of the door, but not in enough time to hear what would come out of Tim's mouth next and bring my entire world crashing down.

Assuming no one was in the room, except Tim and the furniture he had placed in the office, he continued to speak freely. Just as I was one step away from the hallway, what Tim said, which I was not far enough away where I would question what I heard, a devastating secret was revealed.

"You are my wife and if you are willing to fight for us, I'm all in. I've loved you since the beginning and that has not changed."

Infuriated, I forced his office door wide open almost bringing each letter that spelled his name to the ground in shattered pieces. The door that I had entered for months never once with the indication that I was involved with another woman's husband.

Startled to say the least, Tim felt and witnessed my presence as I remained still at the door, face frozen, hands trembling, heart crumbling.

"Married," I shouted.

Phone falling from his ear to the floor, Tim raced over in my direction calling out to me, "Lesley let me explain."

Wanting to run out of the building as fast as I could, my body remained bound to the floor wanting to wake up from this horrible dream. What was he going to possibly explain; pursuing me after refusing his advancements numerous times, lying when asked if he were with anyone, making love without the use of protection knowing the possibilities, not being man enough to be honest, parading me around the shop now feeling like some side hoe, feeding me the same bullshit he was feeding his wife.

The distance all made sense now. We were hot and heavy when they were not and completely cooled off when they rekindled. As if my life weren't already chaotic enough, he knew all that I had been through which I never hid nor denied and the fact that I came to him with an already broken heart, chose to dissolve the remnants of what Trent had yet to destroy.

Rubbing my shoulders, he pleaded with me to sit and listen causing me to shrug my arms to release his hands. My feet, finally able to move, I began to walk backwards out of the door while my head nodded left and right in resentment and disbelief.

I ran out of the building as fast as I could, Tim no longer following and sat in my car where I released the hurt of betrayal and cried out due to someone else's lies; heart shattered, future no longer mattered.

CHAPTER NINETEEN

LOST HOPE

Needing to release my feelings to someone who would not judge my action nor reactions or lack thereof, I vented to my diary whom I had not interacted with in some time. Seeing as though we were becoming strangers towards one another, I filled her in, recounting each and every second leading up to last week when I learned, being in the right place at the right time, that Tim was married, devastation weighing heavy on me.

Barely able to breathe, I felt as though someone had just released a thousand bricks on my chest making this journey now more fearful than I anticipated. I remained inside of a home with a man I did not want, and shut out from the man I thought, wanted me. This baby and I were all alone and his or her father had no idea that they even existed.

I toyed with the idea of delivering the news to Tim through text, but with the wounds still fresh, exchanging words was the last thing I wanted to do. Not to mention, he had yet to reach out in the form of an apology for each and every lie he ever looked me in the eye and told. Through his own admission, unknowing that I was present, he was on board with making things right with his wife which meant that there was no room for me in his life.

It wasn't that I wanted him to make a choice between his wife and I because I knew how sacred vows were even if he didn't and clearly, he did not, but I had become so involved and practically glued to the hip, turning off my feelings was going to be hard as hell even more now that I was carrying his child.

In this entire ordeal, I was the only one made to hurt so much that I started questioning the meaning of life any longer. My marriage was over, but oh how the roles had changed making this non-existent union even more complicated. The more I tried to push away from all that had died between Trent and I, the more he began trying harder to prove that we still had a life left together. I was entirely clouded by the life I had just lost that I gave no energy repairing the foundation Trent had destroyed. I was hanging on by a strand that was transparent and had you not looked close enough, wouldn't even know that it even existed.

In many ways I blamed him for everything I had gone

through and for all that I was now faced to deal with by myself, trying so hard to get him to love and notice me. There was so much damage that had been done at the hands of Trent's past behavior which he acted as though did not exist that I could not allow myself to love again. Men as I knew it and had been exposed to it, were no good and only out for themselves. Neither Trent nor Tim gave a damn about me and I wasn't sure I gave a damn about myself.

All I could think of was what Tim was doing with his wife and with me now out of the picture, how he no longer had to hide or prance around his lies. The guys at his office must have thought that I was a total joke. I could only imagine how many women were coming in and out of his office like a revolving door or how many times he had been present, waiting for a woman in need to extend his business card to appear like a knight in shining armor.

Replaying that very night, oh how I wished I would have just called Trent back instead of allowing Tim to lure me into a business relationship with the intent of a sexual one in which he had no thoughts of making more.

I had to give it to him, he was smooth in all areas. So smooth that I could not blame him either for every detail of this affair which made me even more upset. I could have declined the advancements and stuck by my word, listening to what appeared like my conscience, but were probably my parents telling me to stop, think, and pray the devil away.

If I wasn't depressed enough, I started to also wonder if his wife was pretty. I wondered what she had that I did not, making him want to stay with her. Did she have long beautiful hair? Were her breasts full and noticeable? Were her teeth straight and pearly white? Was her behind to die for? Could she make Tim smile the way that I had? Was she capable of giving Tim a child and being a great mother?

The thought of him making love to me and then going home to her or the other way around, killed me. When he touched me and I touched him, had he previously been with his wife? When he moaned just before climax, was it his wife he envisioned? With every peck to his lips I gave, was it his wife to taste? When he went home at night, was I just a blur in the shadows of his day?

I started to feel as though I was going crazy. One minute I was over Tim and the next I missed him so much. I hated and loved him at the same time and felt this new life of mine that had turned upside down was so unfair. Unlike Stacy, wanting to kill the next woman who admitted pregnancy by her husband, I was not wanting to kill Tim's wife, but I did question the value of my life, seeing as though it had turned to the point of no return.

This just wasn't fair and I now had to live with every consequence to the actions of both Trent and Tim, but could I do it any longer? Did I have the strength to press forward? Could I actually bring this baby into the world where I would have to explain to he or she why their father and I weren't together, how they came to have a step mother that would take the place of their mother in my absence, and how I came to be divorced?

The devil had surely taken the lead in my life and the energy I once had to persevere through anything, had now vanished. I needed someone to save me before my next action was my last.

CHAPTER TWENTY

NO MORE SECRETS

The project that Stacy and I had collaborated on together was a huge success, despite my now emotional instability triggered by both pregnancy hormones and personal attributes. From the looks, that fire and glow Stacy had been demonstrating recently, had burned out as it appeared she was putting on a show just to get through the presentation. I mean the last couple of weeks you couldn't tell Stacy anything. She was so full of life and in great spirits, but upon conclusion of the presentation that shocked everyone as Stacy had proven herself to the nay sayers, she was quiet and distant; something obviously bothering her.

Office manager, extremely proud at the two of us, extended his gratitude by taking the entire floor out for drinks across the street at the local bar. Having revealed to Stacy only, that I was pregnant, I accepted the invitation with no intentions of drinking.

We all gathered our jackets as the weather was warm to touch, but windy as we walked across the street together. Tim, still heavy on my mind as it had now been two weeks since either of us spoke, I tried as hard as I could to get him off of my mind and the best way I knew how to do this was to focus on someone else's problems and who better than Stacy. She was the one that needed a drink after all that she had gone through and I hoped that she would take advantage as our manager was treating.

In walked my coworkers as I waited outside, answering Trent's phone call. Having no romantic involvement or much interaction for that matter, Trent was taking baby steps to get back to the way things used to be, myself, still not impressed.

He had made it a habit to call me in the afternoon to check on my day and see what I wanted for dinner. One would think that he knew I was pregnant with his change in demeanor around the house recently.

Surprisingly, I had found myself coming home for days with an entirely spotless house that Trent took over cleaning. Dinner had been prepared, table set for two his only request to me, "Sit. I'll take your briefcase."

Jasmine Herring's, *More Than Enough*

Assuming it would be loud in the karaoke bar, I took the call outside so that I could hear him clearly. "Hello!"

"Hey Les! I don't mean to disturb your afternoon, but I wanted to check in and see how your presentation went."

He hadn't called me Les since we started dating years ago and his concern for potentially interrupting my day was a new one on me. Who was this man I was speaking to because he was not the Trent that found joy interrupting my day and causing ruckus?

So used to Tim checking on me around this time through text mostly, which I could not deny that I missed, I was completely turned off that it was Trent, but again, appreciating the gesture, I took what I could get, "It actually went well. Thank you for asking!"

It took a lot out of me to continue on with this dialogue that we had involved ourselves in. It was almost as though I had to force my words out, trying not to sound irritated and bored.

Why the urge now to do what I asked of you for months? Could he and Traci have ended their relationship with one another and now he was able to give me his undivided attention? Was he no longer torn between two women, finally deciding to give his all to the marriage he had vowed to commit? I just didn't get what brought on the change and sure did not bother asking.

"I'm glad it went well! Would you like to go out for lunch?"

This would be our first date in four months, but I would have to decline as my boss had already invited me out who I'm sure was now starting to wonder where I was as I had yet to enter into the building. Feeling as though I were being rude to my coworkers, I wrapped the call up, "My boss actually invited us out for drinks to celebrate. I'll just see you when I get home."

Even though the only order I was giving the bartender was a water with lemon, I gave my whereabouts to Trent as I had never had a problem telling him my exact location and at this day in time, did not care what his position was learning that I wasn't coming straight home.

Assuming that there would be some form of argument as I had declined his invite, I was surprised by his response, "You deserve to feel appreciated, but are you going to drink?" Was I going to drink? That was a silly question seeing as though I stated that I was going to a bar and that's what most people do that enter. Maybe he was worried about my driving, but again, having shown no concern before, I guess he was starting to see life moving on without him.

I responded one last time, this time seriously cutting the small talk short, "Trent. I said that I was invited to the bar, not that I was going to drink. I really have to go now."

Letting me go, I placed my phone safely in my purse and walked in to the bar in search of the rest of the party who to sight, had made themselves comfortable, one person on the stage singing Juvenile's *Back That Ass Up* and all, but Stacy, drinking, carrying on in laughter.

With only water in her cup like mine, I leaned in close to her ear as I would have to shout otherwise & commended her performance throughout the project. Seeing a change that she was able to compose through the presentation, thank God as many were waiting for her to break, I asked if she wanted to talk.

Wasting no time, she instantly began speaking.

"It's my husband."

Having heard nothing about him, I wasn't sure what I

was about to learn probing for more, "What about him?"

Scooting closer to me, Stacy now in my ear, responded, "Things had been looking up for us lately. I mean, there was no baby mama drama, he was coming home, and we were even making love the way we used to. Now he's back to his old ways and does not even speak to me. He seems very depressed which I've never seen him behave before and every time I try to get close and extend my love and care for him, he picks a fight and walks away. I feel like I'm losing him again and wonder if his heart is somewhere else."

Well at least this time, he hadn't fathered anymore children not that it was expected, but it was. I looked at Stacy and began to realize that we were so much alike. We were both in a relationship battle by ourselves, seeming to lose. I cried for both she and myself, almost close to revealing to her that I too was going through similar circumstances. Wanting to break to someone human for a change and not blank pages in a notebook, the courage to do so was lacking for this would involve tarnishing my reputation and possibly losing a friend if Stacy did not agree with the way I had handled things in my marriage. Having been cheated on herself, this topic was so close to home that I thought almost positive she would not take well. Used to putting my problems aside, I chose to mend my wounds by trying to fix hers.

"Why does he have to be involved with someone else? I mean you said things were looking up, right? What about the relationship has changed?"

Hands planted on the table, throwing back the water as if it were straight Gin, Stacy laid her reasoning on the table for me to piece together.

"You know that he is no saint and as much as I wanted to give up on us, something told me to stay and that things would get better. God finally answered my prayers, bringing my husband home and consistently at that. He finally started coming home after work, entering into the house in a good mood which he had not done in some time. It was like his life had meaning again. The love making was better than ever and at night I would just watch him lay next to me, sleeping like a peaceful angel, displaying such a beautiful smile. Recently, his old patterns have formed. When he comes home and I do mean when, he is angry, no longer wanting to talk, lay next to me, or even look into my eyes. It is almost like I disgust him. I've even heard him on the other end of the bathroom door and I can hear him crying. When asked if there is anything I can do, he just yells and pushes me away."

I tell you these men and their emotions. Almost forgetting my own internal mountains to bare, for once, I tried to reason with her husband and his recent actions, "That does not mean that it's another woman. Maybe he is going through some personal issues that he is not yet ready to reveal to you. As his wife, you just have to stick by him and be a reminder that you are not his enemy, but his partner in life. Show him how much you love him and want your marriage to work if that is what you really want. Sometimes we have to place our own problems and worries aside to be the strength that our spouse needs. Marriage is no easy job; it takes courage, faith, and most of all, belief in God."

Listening to the empowering words I had given to Stacy, I started rewinding the tape in my own head. As much as I had been ignoring Trent's efforts, he was still making an effort to be the husband that I married. The day we walked down the aisle I recall the pastor telling us that the road ahead although beautiful and full of life to begin, would have its tests that if not grounded as one, would pull us apart and boy had we been failing tests lately.

Turning away from Stacy, both now in opposite directions, I focused in on the current singer on stage and started looking back at my life, reevaluating all that it was currently. Had I invested all that I could in my marriage or had I given up too easily? Pregnant now with another man's child, I began on a path filled with emotion and embarrassment as I knew once Trent learned of the news, even though he did not want children, would hurt him as he was going the extra mile to amend the wrongs he had done for so long, tearing us apart. If he decided not to remain married to me any longer, I feared that due to my actions, he may be scared to trust another woman let alone open up his heart again and I could not live knowing I was the cause.

Asking for the next singer to report on stage, our entire table was wasted, no one able to stand long enough to complete an entire song, but Stacy and I. Looking in the direction of one another, both pointing the finger, I decided to stand and take the lead. I was no Mariah Carey, but did have a church choir background which I attended rehearsal every Wednesday while my parents were in bible study. With it being so early in the afternoon, no one occupied the bar, but the office. Not a soul in the house sober, who would honestly remember whether or not I could hold a note?

Everyone applauding, slurring their chants and pep talks as they vaguely recognized me on stage, I awaited the DJ to pick a song and on the screen showed the title, *Run to You* by

Whitney Houston. As the melody began I instantly felt consumed by emotion as I expressed each note to the crowd.

I took a stance, no longer making excuses and realized that it was me to blame for the problems currently possessed. It wasn't Trent who although had not made our marriage easy, proved that marriage was no walk in the park as our minister had warned. It was not even Tim who had lied and hurt me. I threw the word cheating around for a period of time, but it was I who had cheated as the married party. Tim owed me nothing because there were no vows that bonded us together only a temporary moment of excitement with no promissory terms of how long it would last.

As the song concluded, I dropped the mic leaving the bar with a standing ovation. Hoping to have left Stacy enough guidance to have patience with her husband if in fact she wanted to be with him, I reiterated my words while retrieving my purse.

Walking in to the karaoke bar a broken woman, I left with a new-found purpose.

The ultimate test my husband and I were about to embark upon and may destroy what was slowly being repaired, would be the confession I had to come clean and share. Trent deserved to know that I was pregnant which was not the hard part to share. It was part two that would be the determining factor of our marriage and most fearful. I knew that he would not question whether or not the baby was his as there had been no indication of infidelity on my end seeing as though he was blinded by his own actions, paying no attention to what was right underneath his nose. Nevertheless, I would not keep that a secret although I was unsure of the outcome.

Before coming clean, I would have to enter into God's house for I needed prayer and guidance as to how to go about this mission, what words to say, and how to move forward for there was no easy way in any of this.

Lord give me strength.

STAND BY ME

The time had come and as much as I wished it all away, I had to face my fears head on, no turning back. With morning sickness in full swing, the appearance of my stomach blossoming out, and my appetite on the rise, it was only a matter of time before Trent questioned whether or not I was pregnant. Mentally, I prepared myself for a world that would either forgive and stand by me or leave me and accept not.

Already in awkward form, after tossing and turning all night long, I had awakened to a dream I had not yet learned the meaning of. Out in the distance, I could hear a familiar, somber voice filled with much pain, cry out from a far, "I'm so sorry. Please forgive me." Unable to make out the face or quite recognize the voice, I began to wonder if it were foreshadowing my very own life after revealing to Trent that yes, his suspicions that I may be pregnant were true and no, he was not the father. Would I find myself apologizing for the rest of my life or would he have it in his heart to accept my apology, which I was courageous enough to extend, moving forward with this child as its step father and not biological? Not expecting that he would remain as this was asking a bit much, my hope was that he would at least welcome the attempt to try and reconcile as everyone makes mistakes.

This dream brought me to cold sweats as the only ending was the woman drifting off into a cloudy distance that was unknown which is the way that my life seemed to be settling. The future was unclear and although I could put off what needed to be outed, for each day I neglected to speak the truth, I would continue to carry a burden that added an additional layer of stress to my already troubled life.

Whatever was to come of this day, I had already accepted as so and prayed that God would give me strength for the things that were no longer in my control. It was my faith and trust in him that was going to see me through this mountain that I had no choice, but to cross on my own.

Preparing for church, I could hear commotion ringing from the bedroom closet and as I tiptoed towards the door, barely opened, I could see Trent sitting on the floor, Indian style. Confused, I was not exactly sure what he was up to and why he remained in a room filled with clothes and shoes, observing not a single item. With a subtle knock to alert him that I was preparing to enter in as he was blocking the door, aside he moved and what I witnessed next, was a sight seen never before.

In plain view, Trent had in his hands our wedding album from nine months ago which he finally laid his hands on for the very first time. Pretending as though I did not notice that he was in fact crying while sifting through each page of what was once a happier time, I detoured to my side of the closet where I began sorting through my dresses in search of the right one to wear for church.

Reaching for my jewelry box on the top shelf, down fell an earring sitting on top of the box which happened to land near Trent. While I stood searching, Trent remained in a seated position and what I saw as he leaned backwards to grab my earring he found near a pair of shoes, took the breath out of my almost lifeless body.

Having not once taken a moment to view the wedding collection with me as this was not a priority of his, I always knew that my diary would remain safely kept, out of the public eye, hidden in the very box Trent laid not a single finger print. As he leaned back to grab my earring, tucked under his right thigh was the untold truth, housed in my diary I never thought would be in the position of compromise. Not sure whether or not he had opened and read all that I was preparing to share, he uttered not one word from the time I stepped foot in the closet.

Wanting not to draw attention to the fact that I noticed my possession now in his, the diary that would paint a disheartening picture of a dark past, I left in the hands of Trent. It was he who would ultimately make the decision to ignore the for better or worst part of our vows or stand the test.

Excusing myself from the area we both occupied, church clothes in hand, I got dressed as fast as I could to avoid the inevitable truth and left, for the first time ever, without asking Trent to tag along for church service.

Barely able to catch my breath once outside as I had almost met my fate while home, I kept thinking of what I should and could have said while the opportunity presented itself. Then my mind started exploring. Maybe he hadn't read my diary after all. Maybe he just removed it out of the way as it was on top of the album cover. Maybe he respected my privacy enough, that had it been opened, he would have closed it the moment he noticed that my inner thoughts, dating as far back

Jasmine Herring's, *More Than Enough*

241

as the first moment I felt unwanted by Trent, well before Tim was even in the picture, were locked inside. The more I drove myself crazy in thought, reality hit me; there was nothing private in a marriage let alone a home that we shared together and so my maybes became certainties.

Certain, that had he not yet begun to take in all that my diary was about to shockingly confess, he would now as I had exited the building. Allowing life to take its course, I left both he and the white pages which contained many scenes you'd only view in a movie or read in a novel to become exposed.

Lured in the front door by the sweet melody of Christ Temple's church choir, I immediately wanted to fall to my knees at the front of the sanctuary as I was overwhelmed, feeling God's presence drawing near. It was something about being in the house of the Lord that allowed all that weighed heavy to release itself into God's hands and somewhat free you, turning worry into faith.

I tell you, party of one always granted you the VIP seating section. Placed front and center in the direct eyesight of Pastor Jordan Xavier who was no stranger to telling it like it was, sugar coating absolutely nothing. The way his messages were set up, you were guaranteed in some way, shape, or form to grasp something from his sermon and apply it for your good.

Just as the musicians lowered their keystrokes, which was cue that the pastor was preparing to speak, the choir positioned themselves in their seating arrangements and the entire congregation stood, applauding as Pastor Xavier stood before the podium. Lead by the spirit, it took one shout of, "AMEN," to bring the choir back to song and a praise break to follow. Myself included, I began to nod and clap my hands along with the crowd, pumping myself up for a powerful word that would direct my life and place it all into perspective.

"Has the Lord been good to you," asked Pastor Xavier.

From each pew, you could hear fellow members respond, "YES!"

Repeating the question for those whose response unconvincing, "I said, has the Lord been

good to you?"

Asking each of us to open our bibles, we were introduced to Matthew 15:13-14 and out came the title for today's word, *Lost Sight, but You Gon Be Alright.*

The passage was read as the congregation followed and after, a prayer was spoken to bless the upcoming word, "Lord, I thank you for each and every individual who came this morning to hear a word from you. I ask right now father that you touch these hearts in a very special way. Someone right here and right now is going through a storm that has the road ahead cloudy and uncertain, but with a word from you, lost sight will be no more. Amen."

With a hand gesture, Pastor Xavier motioned for us all to sit as he prepared to deliver what was sure to speak life into someone's soul, "Take your seats."

Completely silent and with a look as though he were getting clarification from God, pastor jumped from three stairs off of the pulpit, smile now present on his face. He was known for his animated tactics to get one's attention, "Did anybody come for a word this morning?"

Many shouted, already moved with the spirit inside, "YES LORD."

Back row filled with late comers who had no shame, shouting, "AMEN."

Sister Pat delivering an unchanged high-pitched

response as always, waved her bulletin, used as a fan, back and forth, "ALRIGHT NOW."

Hands raised, arms extended, and at the edge of our seats, we strapped on our safety belts and opened up our heart and ears as pastor began delivering the message the Lord sent him to offer to his people.

As he pointed and looked almost in my direction, Pastor Xavier said, "Someone in this very room is going through some major life changes that has their future filled with doubt and fear."

No matter how many sermons I listened to, each and every message I heard directly applied to my current status. Sometimes I felt like I was the lucky one to hit the lottery and that there was no one else in the sanctuary, but me, the pastor, and God's Word.

Praying that he would make sense of my current situations, unaware what I was battling, God did and sent the message to be delivered to me through His fellow servant who had a calling of ministry on his life.

Walking back up to the pulpit, pastor sat the microphone down and inserted an ear piece that would allow him freedom to release his hands and walk back and forth as he too was moved by his very own words as he spoke life to each of us.

"Anyone felt so far into a situation that you thought no hopes of ever coming out? That the world as you knew it kept moving, but you remained in the same position unsure whether to turn left or right or if either option would have a light at the end of the tunnel?"

Not wanting to draw attention to myself or make it obvious that I was the person he was describing, I kept my praises to a minimum. The Lord knew my heart and therefore there was no need to share in my personal praise.

Pastor Xavier went on to conclude that we must attack the problems we allow to hinder our lives by giving them to the Lord. That if we stand still on our own, we will continue to drown in our own sorrow. That in order to come out on top and with a clear focus, we must accept what it is that has occurred, pray for better days, and move forward with our heads held high, allowing the Lord to lead us. It is only then that we will be alright.

This message, although shorter than his normal which

I'm sure many were thankful, was just what I needed to place my life into perspective. I had lost sight long ago of my marriage and it was my interactions with Tim that blocked all that my husband and I could be. It was my yearn for love and affection when I felt I needed it that allowed me to keep my marriage hanging in the clouds. It was myself, committing adultery, that forced my life to spiral out of control. It was my urgency to have the life I wanted, when I wanted, that lack of patience brought so much pain and heartache.

On point with his message and having not stopped for one water break, in spite of being out of breath and covered in sweat, Pastor Xavier moved service along, extending the alter call.

"Someone in the audience came here today not sure of the next step to take in their life. I am here to tell you today that although the road may seem scary and ye may not know the outcome, you need courage to persevere and prayer to eliminate your fear. Stand and allow the Lord to lead you as you make your way to the alter."

Before he could even invite those to give their lives to Christ, a handful of members led by a powerful word, walked up to the front of the sanctuary, ready to give their lives to

Christ.

Hand outstretched, pastor extended his invitation, "The doors of the church are open."

Swaying back and forth, not sure whether or not to stand in agreement, I watched as others took the leap of faith, awaiting a sign that I too should head to the alter for prayer as much was needed.

Standing to my feet, I became consumed with pain as I thought of the day of my wedding and the words spoken by my father just before he escorted me down the aisle. As much as I tried to be a big girl and hide how nervous I was to become someone's wife, my father, knowing his one and only daughter, like a dog to a person untrusting of the animal, could smell the fear miles away and spoke life into my soul.

Looking directly into my eyes, he held my hand and said, "Sweetheart. This independent act you have forever held onto ends today. As you and Trent join as one, your life, his life, are no longer your own. You two will be one and this means that no matter what one or the other faces, you must stand together, pray together, no matter how tough the challenge may be and there will come a time it all seems impossible. There is nothing you can do alone, but with God as your shield, your marriage will be unbreakable."

Just as he spoke these words into my life, he prayed for us and told me how proud of his little girl he was. That was the last heartfelt conversation that I had with my father and I wondered while he was staring down at me from heaven, if he could still state that he was proud of me, considering all that I had done to break a union that lacked so much.

I began to cry out, searching for God as I needed him now, no longer ashamed or afraid to admit it. No more was I going to continue with the facade like my life was perfect. I wanted to tackle each and every obstacle head on, make my peace with every situation that weighed heavy on my heart, and look up to a clear future for myself, my child, and hopefully my husband; if he would still have me.

Feeling the weights being removed from my shoulders one by one, I turned to my left to excuse myself as I walked past the person sitting next to me. No longer caring what anyone thought, I walked down the aisle, ready to position my life in a better direction.

Asking the crowd to touch the hand of their neighbor, I

could feel a hand grab hold of mine just as I bowed my head and closed my eyes. Although this person knew not what I was dealing with and I knew nothing of my neighbor, I squeezed his or hers as directed by the pastor and held on to each word the pastor prayed.

"Turn to your neighbor and give them a hug of encouragement."

I opened my eyes that were still filled with tears, but this time, the tears were of joy as this day presented new meaning and direction. Today I would speak truth to my husband, no matter the outcome and also reveal to Tim what I had been torn to share since learning that he too was married. Wiping my eyes, I turned to my neighbor following the direction of pastor and the sight before my eyes was breath taking.

In front of me, dressed in a suit and tie with open arms was my husband, Trent. If this moment hadn't given me enough courage to press forward, Trent being here by my side moved enough to come to church in search of me, was a feeling I simply could not explain.

I treasured this day as I held on for dear life. This was a moment; holding hands, standing in the same vicinity of one another without argument, heads bowed as we conversed with God, we had not shared in some time. Devotion began in my head and I asked God to please grant us many more moments such as this one even after all was said and done. That if in fact, we were closing in on the final hours of our lives together, as a married party, may this memory be lasting forever more in our hearts.

CHAPTER TWENTY-TWO

TOGETHER AGAIN

Pulling up to the driveway alongside my husband after church concluded, I remained in my car, reflecting on the breath-taking moments this morning. Trent surprising me at church was one of the highlights of the day as I had extended the invitation for months only to find the invitation declined and myself, alone at the alter praying that one day, he would see fit to join me. Just when I thought the day could not get any better, not only had Trent decided to visit Christ Temple, but had made the ultimate decision to give his life to Christ once the doors of the church were open.

Thinking that I could not shout any louder standing by his side, I continued to give thanks to God for moving in my husband. What he did next, placed me into a total state of disbelief while dropping to my knees.

Without notion, Trent had made prior arrangements with the pastor, to speak in front of all members of Christ

Temple and lay his burdens down while staring into my eyes. Extremely apologetic and heartfelt, Trent explained that he had not been the best husband that he should have been to me, giving a few examples to paint a clear picture, the confession more powerful, and vowed that he was going to do all he could to rebuild the foundation he came to terms with, knowing he was tearing down.

It was not like Trent to ever admit fault in any situation let alone tell the world, but on this day, he did and it was his courage to admit his part that gave me a boost of energy to confess my very own as he had no idea all that I had done.

Preparing to open the door for me as he waited near the driver side, I cut the car off, but not before hearing a pop ricochet underneath the hood. With great caution, I removed the key out of the ignition and met Trent halfway, opening my door. With great urgency, Trent demonstrated his eagerness to find the source of the sudden pound underneath the car's hood.

Recalling the day, I needed his assistance with the car I remained helpless in the grocery store parking lot, I pondered on how life would have been had I put my pride aside, called Trent back after our dispute, and admitted that I needed him. Had he come, I would never have had a need for Tim and he would have found some other female to prey upon. Regardless, I too played a role, unable to fault either man entirely and took in Trent's willingness here and now, with complete gratitude. Having no mechanical background, Trent vowed to have the car looked at, "I'll take this in first thing in the morning. I don't want you two in a compromising position where I cannot be there for you."

What did he mean by you two? I looked at him as he remained crouched down on the ground unknowing of what he just said. Taking a few steps back, I placed the bible carried in my hand, in front of my stomach to hide the tiny bump that to the eye was noticeable, to more than just myself possibly.

Jumping up from the ground, closing the hood, Trent walked towards me, wiping his hands together to remove the engine debris and said, "I'm sorry. I meant that I did not want you in harm's way," aiming for my stomach which was blocked, holding on to my side instead.

"Let's go inside. I have a surprise for you."

Walking in behind Trent, I started to become very suspicious of the things he may know about me still not certain whether or not he read my diary. What surprise would he have for me; divorce papers, my bags packed, another woman waiting to take my place, my diary on the kitchen table with a knife through it?

Standing at the front door, wanting to hide no more, I looked back out towards the street questioning whether or not to make a final run away from my problems or face them head on. As I took one step down the stairs that lead to the bottom of our front porch, I was greeted by the gentle hand of Trent whom I did not see coming my way as I was looking back and escorted me in the house,

"Come on Baby."

It was here that I knew God was telling me to walk forward, looking back no more.

I swear, the nicer Trent became the harder it was to come clean knowing that I was going to break his heart. The heart that I was finally getting to know for the better.

Hand in hand, Trent took me inside of our living room where he had our wedding frozen still on the flat screen TV, replaying the day we said I do. Trailing me to the couch, I was guided to the cushion of the sofa where I sat and he kneeled. The next thing I knew, my shoes were off, feet in the air, and there Trent was, massaging each and every toe like I had become accustomed of doing to his after a hard day's work.

With no fond memories, all I recalled of this couch were the countless times I had introduced a warm plate of food he so angrily rejected, the nights I waited up for him to return home unsure of who he was with or where he had been, the disappointing times he would come home inebriated and want to argue, and how could I ever forget, the times he wanted to unromantically have sex out of simple urge where it lasted no more than two and a half minutes. To witness a pleasant moment like this, one I had prayed we may one day share, I simply counted my blessings and thanked God for what may seem like a tiny moment to some, but for me, everything.

Pausing for a moment to press play on the television, Trent excused himself from the living room area, stating that he would return shortly. Lifting up from the couch, almost forgetting that I had some things to get off of my chest, I sat up from a reclined position, removed both hands from my stomach as I was not going to hide my pregnancy any longer, and waited for Trent to reunite with me inside of the living room where a Tell All was preparing to debut.

My hands and legs trembling, Trent welcomed himself

back into my presence, smiling from a far as he watched with one eye, an angle of the ring bearer, who was his cousin's son, walk down the aisle with our rings just before we said I do. The smile on his face hurt me to the core knowing I was about to remove it and make him feel as though his hard work and want to change for the better was a wasted desire.

Breathing heavily, body now restless, I paused no more, "Trent. There are some things that I need to tell you."

Smiling still, Trent reached his hand out, grabbed mine, and asked, "Would you come with me please?"

Clearly, he did not hear me when I said that I needed to talk to him.

Nudging me towards the dining room, I pulled back and said for the second time, more serious than the first, "Please Trent. Let me get this out," surrendering with my hands outstretched.

In a stand still position, Trent turned, holding my hand no more, and responded, hand on his chest as if he were now pleading, "Would you allow me to start first? Please?"

As if I had not waited long enough to remove the weights

that were sinking me to the lowest level, I would now be forced to wait even longer which granted me another attempt to run from my past just to accommodate Trent's yearn to speak first.

Feeling defeated, I agreed to allow Trent the platform, "Sure Trent. You first."

What was so important that he could not wait? I guess I was about to find out.

Grabbing a hold of my hand again, Trent walked me in to the dining room where dinner was prepared, a card placed on the table, and a jewelry box lay on the plate in front of the chair I would typically sit.

Trent now in front of me, pulled out my chair, reached his hand out, and asked me to sit carefully. Pushing me up to the table, he asked that I not read nor open any of the items in front of me until he said what was on his heart. Taking in the scenery, I watched as Trent walked over to the sound system nearby and began Luther Vandross's, *Here and Now* to be heard throughout the entire house.

What made this moment special was that this was the very song we danced as we were introduced as a married couple in front of our family and friends. Of course, the tears came as this day was getting harder and harder for me to tell all that would put moments like this to a halting end.

Pulling up a chair next to me, Trent asked, "Would you open the card?"

Reaching towards the table, I removed the card from the envelope it was kept and the outside read, "If I had one wish it would be that I meet you sooner and had longer to love you." The inside read, "Lesley for all that I ever put you through, I want to say that I am truly and deeply sorry and vow to spend the rest of my life making up each day a tear was shed, your heart was broken, and a smile was removed from your beautiful face."

Unable to contain my emotions, the tears positioned themselves front and center and to my aid was the man of my past whom I had grown to love and cherish, wiping my tears away with both hands, now leaning forward to place his lips, recently unfamiliar, on my forehead.

Holding on to his hands while they rested on both sides of my face, we both found ourselves interrupted by my phone which continued to go off for approximately five minutes. Remaining inside of my purse which I had left by the door to allow Trent access to my hand, I could not comprehend who was in such desperation of my assistance that they did not understand me not answering meant that I was busy. Wanting to live in the moment, I ignored whoever was in need for this day was of the utmost importance and nothing or no one else mattered. The caller would have to learn to take matters into their own hands without Lesley today.

Calling out from the kitchen, "Baby, I forgot something. I'll be right back."

Wondering now if Trent was intentionally running away from my words for fear of ruining the moment or learning something he thought may be hard to swallow, I tried one final time to stop him before he walked out of the door, shouting from the dining room chair, "TRENT. WAIT. DON'T GO."

Brief sigh, head down, Trent had vanished and my opportunity disappeared, exiting stage right along with my husband.

Not sure where he was headed or how long he would be away, I entered into our living room, but not before passing by the mirror that rested on the wall behind our couch. I glanced at myself, shadow looking back at me and remained quiet and still. In a few short months, I was going to be someone's mother and could not help, but to feel a connection with my unborn child as I rubbed my stomach from top to bottom and declared that I was not going to allow a few interferences to keep me from telling the truth. I owed my child the chance at a decent life; one not built on lies that I would have to answer for later. Since every attempt failed to inform my husband, maybe it was a sign that I should go and speak with Tim first.

Without even the smallest greeting of hello, Tim and I had refrained from any conversation with one other and as much as it hurt in the beginning, I had come to terms with a life no longer involving a man who once took my pain away. So clouded by my desires, I had come to realize that I was using Tim as a crutch and he for lust. There was no love amongst us, only lies in which our spouses were unaware.

Time to spare, I toyed with the idea of making my last and final visit to the very shop that began this path of deceit and pain. Not sure what state of mind Tim was in since the conclusion of our affair, who would be present upon my unannounced arrival, or if he would even welcome my presence. None of these things mattered. All I knew was Trent was returning home and not sure exactly how much time remained, this trip had to be fast, to the point, and never again.

My only hope was that once I revealed to Tim the news, there would be no accusations or questioning whether or not he was the only potential father or altercations as this blow may come as a surprise at the wrong time.

Get in and get out was my mission and I was sticking to it.

CHAPTER TWENTY-THREE

BABY WATCH OUT

The longer I sat in the car in front of Tim's shop, the more influenced I became as something in my head was telling me to turn around and go back home to my husband. Most likely God speaking to me and out of all the other times he had probably given me a sign to go home, on this day it almost felt as if he were shouting it directly into my ear. Not to mention, the double doors that allowed you entry into the building were bordered up for some odd reason, making this visit even more awkward.

With no cars in the front parking lot, I became suspicious if anyone was present and took a drive behind the building, still remaining in the car. My mind replaying the many times I had driven to the back wondering why I never realized that we were and would always be a hidden lie. I guess when you are down so low and in need that bad, you become blinded and willing to accept any and all temporary remedies until it becomes plain, usually by some form of hurt, that the person

Jasmine Herring's, *More Than Enough*

you're involved, is no good for you.

Back door cracked, I contemplated one last time whether or not I was going to go inside in search of my former lover. His car was the only one parked behind the building, but why the back door was open, Tim nowhere in sight, I could only imagine what I may walk into or who he was waiting for. Taking the key out of the ignition, I swung the driver door open, extending one leg out and then the other, stood tall with the courage of a lion and walked with my head held high, reentering the back door, one final time.

Voice trailing down the hall, I could hear Tim in a rage and with my conscience saying, "Get Out," I did not allow what I thought fear and the devil to stop me in my tracks. Watching Tim stomp back and forth, observing no one else in the room, I made my presence known by standing in the middle of the floor, awaiting eye contact; purse and keys attached closely to my body.

As an end to his rampage, Tim threw his phone across the room as a means to release the anger clearly built inside and although I did not care of his internal issues, it was a sight I had seen only once before, this case, the most severe.

Appearing to turn around no time soon, I made the call out to Tim to seek his attention and speak my piece, "TIM."

His breath up and down at a fast pace, my voice seemingly recognizable, without turning to face me, Tim spoke back, "Lesley?"

At least I could check off the list that he was not waiting for someone else because had he been that dumb to call out my name without looking as he was waiting on another female, he may have gotten more than he bargained for.

Focused entirely, I responded in the form of a specific agenda, "I need to speak with you."

Turning in my direction, Tim began to walk over and in my head, instant snap shots of what transpired each and every time he came my way caused a reaction to take five steps backwards. This was not an intimate call, there was no buttering me up, and I most certainly was not going to lose focus of this very important mission.

Attempting to avoid looking directly into his eyes, afraid of giving off any wrong signals that may mislead him, I looked down instead and noticed that Tim's hand was dripping with blood. Either in shock or unaware himself, I made reference to what appeared to be some form of a cut, "Your hand."

Confusion written all over his face, Tim asked, "What about my hand?"

Not sure how he could miss it or more obvious, why he did not feel the wound, "It's bleeding."

Hand drenched in blood, firsthand witness to enraged behavior entering into the shop, not to mention the front door bordered shut, it was clear that something was going on, but what?

Sitting him down, thinking in my head, no matter what anger or resentment towards this man, he was my child's father and I couldn't just let him bleed to death. I searched the office I was familiar, and found bandages to wrap his hand while inquiring the dark and gloomy vibe that surrounded the entire building, "What happened to the front door?"

Anger flaring back up, I could see his nostrils and eye brows rise while his chest stuck out, "Someone broke in through the front. My guess is that they tried to steal the new shipment of rims we got in last night. This car kept creeping up back and forth in the front parking lot and I thought nothing of it until this morning. Damn man."

That explained the front door, but not his hand bleeding.

"And your hand?"

Snatching it out of my lap as I was one tie away from a finished bandage, Tim stood from the chair and said, "I'm fine."

Why had I even bothered opening the door of conversation? I just didn't know how to turn off my care for the world, always putting myself last. Tim must have thought that I was going to buy that response, taking his word that he was truly fine. Out of all the times I had socialized with Stacy, I knew that when a person said they were fine and the behaviors did not match, they were anything, but fine. Tim was not and although I had not forgotten why I was here, what led to this day, or the fact that I needed to hurry home, I had a heart and the best way to fully get over someone that hurt you was to extend it. Let them see you in a bright light hoping that your light shining would place a better feeling inside of them to want to change, grow, and do better by the next person.

Walking over to Tim, I placed my hand on his shoulder to gain his attention, "Tim, you are not fine."

Repeating myself I asked, "What happened to your hand?" I guess it was my motherly instinct coming out that wanted so bad to nurture the internal issues that at first, I did not care.

Taking back the shoulder I held hostage with my right hand, with an attitude, ignoring my kind gestures, Tim asked with a high-pitched voice, "What do you care Lesley?"

What made him believe that he was the least bit deserving of an attitude towards me? Had he forgotten the heartache he caused? Had he forgotten the lies he told to get what he wanted? I can guarantee that not one tear was shed on his behalf and the nerve of him to disregard my concern.

I was starting to wonder if he was even worthy of knowing that I was carrying his baby. The more it was put into perspective that Tim was the man I had unintentionally selected as the father of this child inside of me, the more upset I became. So upset that I decided to keep my mouth shut and just leave, "You know what Tim? You're right. I don't care."

Throwing my hands in the air as a sign that I was done, I got up, turned the other cheek, and left.

I walked out of the door, but you know we as women had to speak our final thoughts before our grand exit, "Enjoy the rest of your life making others miserable while you go on as if everything is fine."

Disgusted I was. I should have listened to the signs that said not to even step foot into the building, but wanting to be the bigger person, I attempted to extend the olive branch and look where that got me. Here I was, the only one getting worked up and emotional and to think, I was still allowing Tim to get the best of me.

Looking at the time on my phone to calculate how long I had actually been gone, I completely forgot someone had been attempting to contact me as I was reminded by twelve unread text messages along with two voicemails. Gone for what felt like an hour was only seven minutes; the longest seven minutes and wanting not to waste another second of my life with Timothy McWilliams, I continued towards the back door that I left cracked as it was originally.

Making my way out of the door, I could see the light of freedom seep into the building and as it appeared brighter the closer I got and with each step I took, an echo of Tim's voice bounced off the walls entering directly into my eardrum, "I'm so messed up Lesley."

Turning my head around, raising my nose up as if there

were a distinctive odor in the building, he could not seriously deem those words an apology. If it was, I was not buying nor was I impressed. Taking not one step or looking up to determine if his appearance matched his emotions, I gave my undivided attention to each message that appeared to be left by Stacy, curious as to what was so important that she had to inundate both my inbox and mailbox.

From the first to the final message, darkness lifted from each piercing word that mirrored from the screen of my phone to my eyes which absorbed, "After requesting a copy of text messages from the cellphone company, waiting, hoping, and praying to find nothing alarming, I learned that he never stopped cheating. After begging me to trust him, he still maintained a relationship elsewhere."

It was almost a relief having heard nothing about Stacy's husband for as long as I had, but here we were back to reality and from the texts to follow, reality had finally slapped Stacy in the face and it did not appear that she was taking it well.

"Do you think she's prettier than me Lesley?"

"Lesley please pick up."

"What reason do I have to live any longer?"

Jasmine Herring's, *More Than Enough*

"Should I confront him?"

"Why did he break my heart?"

"I feel so dumb."

"I'm so fucking angry."

"I'm going to KILL that bitch."

"She took my husband and I am going to take her life."

"LESLEY??????????"

"You must be busy, but I want you to know that all of my pain will be over today."

Phone in hand, I could not help, but cry out for I was not sure what Stacy was up to. What made it even worse was that I had called her twice, her phone going straight to voicemail.

Tim noticing my slightly distorted appearance, came running just before my knees buckled and into his arms I had fallen, no energy to detach his arms from around my body, "Lesley. Come into my office and catch your breath."

I needed to go back to my husband and also determine

Stacy's whereabouts, but I was in such shock, I could not move. For a second or two, it was like Stacy's words had taken the life right out of my body, myself unable to breath, move, or get my thoughts together.

Unthawing my frozen body consumed with guilt, fear, and the unknown as it pertained to Stacy, Tim's voice, a muffle to my ears asked, "Lesley what's wrong?"

Distracted, unable to make out each word Tim spoke, I contemplated calling the police, but with such little information to give, there wouldn't be much they could do. I did not know where Stacy lived. As many times as she had mentioned her husband, never once did she state his name. All I could do was say a prayer in my head and ask God to deliver Stacy from the years of pain I knew that she had endured and free her from whatever hold her husband had on her to make Stacy feel that she had no other option, but to stay, now so far gone that she wanted to take a life.

Looking at Tim, saying not a single word, I became upset for he was the very man Stacy's husband was and I immediately became disgusted, taking a stand for all women ever hurt by betrayal and deceit. Here Stacy was ready to take the life of a woman her husband had cheated with, unknowing that her husband was most likely lying to the other women he messed around. All Stacy knew was that another woman was in the very spot she fought to hold first rank, now that position was threatened. What I could not understand was why we as women were so quick to attack the other female, who often times was just as innocent believing each and every lie the man spoke. This was probably a portion of what Tim's wife was going through if she even knew that he had cheated. If only I could tell her that I was sorry for her husband's deceit and that I had no idea he was a married Man until after it was too late.

Darkness entering into my heart just looking at Tim, it was time to vacate the building and for good.

"Tim, I have to go."

Attempting to rise from my seat, Tim sat me back down asking five more minutes of my time which at first I thought, boy please.

Looking into his eyes; however, I captured what I felt as true sincerity and granted five remaining minutes of my time, knowing I probably shouldn't have, "Five minutes Tim and then I'm leaving."

Pulling a chair up next to me, Tim attempted to hold my

hands. The last I checked, I wasn't an elderly woman longing for comfort, I was not his child, and certainly not his wife which made the slightest reach for my hand, unjustifiable. The last I remembered, the sense of touch was not required for a conversation to take place.

I quickly pulled away, reminding him with my actions that talking was the only activity we were going to embark upon, jerking my hand back, "Tim you said talk. That's it."

Placing his hands on his lap, understanding that the boundaries crossed before were never to occur again.

"I lied about my involvement with another woman."

He said, "another woman," as if he weren't referring to his wife. I was not sure what type of relationship they had, but I knew that she at least deserved some form of respect and the way he mouthed the word wife was as though he were forced to even call her that upon a choice he made to take her hand in marriage.

Rambling on, I still had not heard the apologetic expression of an I'M SORRY roll off of his tongue. I had been waiting on an apology for over a month now and the way this conversation was going, I felt as though I would never ever receive one. With four minutes left, I wasn't holding my breath, only my keys, purse, and phone, ready to G.O.

"The day I laid eyes on you, I saw a beautiful, but helpless woman who just needed someone to be there for her. I saw my cue to run in and be that man for you and so I took it, knowing that I was married, but never did I plan to take things as far as they went. The more I learned about you and your husband, I knew that we had been brought together for a reason beyond just fixing your car. What you didn't know because I tried as hard as I could to hide it, was that I was broken too."

Here I am listening to a man feed me BS and the nerve of him to fix his lips to gain some sympathy was unbelievable. For someone who actually did the breaking of another's heart that did not belong to him, how could he even fathom brokenness?

Rolling my eyes at the thought of his words even more lies, my ears remained open, but for two and a half more minutes as my feet were about to start walking.

Standing up, Tim got on his knees and made a confession from what he said was his inner soul crying out all he had been afraid to truly own up to, "The way I feel for you stands so much greater than the feelings I have ever felt for my wife. I love you so much. This past month without you made me want to die inside knowing that I hurt you. I thought that once you walked away, I could focus on my marriage, but I couldn't get you off of my mind. Constant reminders of you made me realize that all I had been searching for was in you Lesley."

I could only imagine how many women had heard these lines before. I felt even worse for his wife knowing she was probably at home waiting on him to show, assuming that things were perfect between she and her husband on account of his cowardliness not to confess what was making him stray away.

"She became pregnant very young and wanting to step up and be a man, I married her, but I was not in love. I thought that if I stayed long enough, the love would come, but it never did and I became comfortable. For so long I've searched for a way out without hurting her and then I meet you and for once, I lost sight of any problems I had at home. With you, I was able to start over with someone that meant so much to me. It ate me up inside knowing that you were married and that another man was where I wanted to be. I'm not afraid to say this as men often hide behind pride, but I have been physically sick and lost without you in my life."

Jasmine Herring's, *More Than Enough*
276

Standing up next to Tim, I placed my hand to his lips to silence them. I wanted to hear no more for fear of falling again. Our time together almost up, I wanted to say what I needed to and be done with this charade.

"Tim, I need you to stop speaking and let me say what brought me here today."

Kissing the finger I had placed on his lips, moments of the past secretly depicted in my head. I removed my finger and was startled by what sounded like the back door slam shut.

"Did you hear that?"

Looking dead into my eyes, having not removed himself from the same spot that made me jump from the sound, "It was probably just the wind."

Moving closer to me, "What is it that you need to say," as if we were channeling some brief moment of chemistry.

Clearly two different thoughts in our heads, Tim's eyes full of dreams and possibilities, mine carrying a confessional soul, waited no longer and revealed what our secret affair welcomed us, "Tim, I'm pregnant."

Giving off a sigh of relief as one of the two men in my life finally knew the truth, I waited on a response, not sure what it was going to be. Part of me wanted him to be angry and deny the child, hoping that with all the love my husband had recently shown, he would look past my faults and step up in Tim's place. This was certainly wishful thinking, but a hope I held on to as I prepared to walk out of Tim's life for good and head home to hopefully a more blissful one for Trent and I.

Finally, able to move, Tim took a brief stroll around his desk, planting his feet firm to the ground and looked at me with a smile on his face. No words, only a large grin.

Making it clear in case he did not hear me as he continued in a state of pure serenity, I relayed the message again, louder than the first "Tim. Did you hear me? I said I AM HAVING YOUR BABY."

Fully aware that he heard me the second time stated, what began as a gigantic smile was swiftly turned into a look of shock, fear, and ultimate surprise.

As if running for the final play in a football game, Tim lunged at me, myself now fearful, and shouted from across the room with his arms outstretched, "Lesley. Baby WATCH OUT."

"POP. POP. POP............"

TIM

CHAPTER TWENTY-FOUR

PAIN NO MORE

"911, what is your emergency?"

The moment finally presenting itself, one in which I had prayed for and thought may never arrive, had come, for me to correct my wrongdoings and make amends with the woman I had hurt and betrayed who no longer believed that what we shared was ever genuine.

Never wanting to hurt or bestow upon her any further pain than she had already endured in her life, I had done everything wrong and wanted so much to make it all right again.

All the things I should have, could have, and needed to confess were now compromised and if I did not act fast, into those precious eyes, I may never get to soothe the hurt caused by my selfishness and inability to step up and be the man that she needed, if she would even have me.

Frantic, I begged for the operator to send help, "Please

hurry. She's been shot."

Running towards my office door, afraid that the intruder may hear me and realize that he had only shot one of us, I quickly shut and locked us both inside. Pleading with the dispatcher to send someone to Lesley's aid as she had begun to choke on her very own blood in front of me, I could do nothing, but watch with the eye, stare, and just ask why. Hadn't she been through enough already and yet again, she stood front and center on the battleground, fighting for her life as she had fought for her marriage and for someone to just love and be there for her in a similar form that she had been to everyone else.

Asking question after question, I feared that the EMT's were steady wasting what little time they actually had and would find themselves unable to save the woman I loved and knew that I could not live without even if just a friend. I mean, there was still so much I needed to get off of my chest and the fact that I now knew she was carrying my child, made the stakes even greater. I could not lose Lesley again or miss the opportunity to show and prove that I could be a great father and strong support.

"Sir? I need you to calm down and tell me who's been

shot?"

Begging Lesley to stay with me as her breaths were getting shorter, her eyes weaker, closing shut for periods at a time, and skin cold to touch, I held on to her as tight as I could placing one arm around hers, the other on our child, and began to pray for hers and the strength of our unborn as time was not on our side.

For the life of me, I could not understand why anyone would want to harm such a beautiful woman. To deliberately shoot her three times, was an act I could not comprehend. Whatever it is they had come for, I would have given, putting up not a single fight. I would have even traded places with Lesley and my unborn son or daughter and stood directly in front of the barrel of the gun just so she would not have to fight any longer in a world where her only request was to be loved with a response and return of pure mistreatment.

Asking a second time as I had ignored the first inquiry, through the speaker of my phone, the operator attempted to gain further information, "Assistance is on the way sir. Can you tell me who did this?"

If only I knew. All I could do was give a vague

recollection. The entry to my office a surprise visit, shooting at random, and fleeing the building as I believed they had, I was left with only pieces and rapid snapshots to retell.

Wearing a face mask to cover any distinguishing features or further reveal his ethnicity, the assailant was unknown. Without even the visual of his eyes covered by a black hoodie, the clear image of a shiny silver pistol was the only descriptive figure I could accurately give.

Startled at the sound of a forced gasp of air, I looked down to witness all movement had ceased from Lesley's body, and it was at this moment where I knew that if the EMT's weren't here now, they would be left with a beautiful, but lifeless Lesley who was with us no more.

Wasting no more time on the phone as the sense of urgency had already been addressed, I dropped my cellphone to the ground and began calling out, "LESLEY? LESLEY BABY WAKE UP."

The tears, unable to hold back, I brought Lesley's feather weight body towards my chest where I squeezed her tight, selfishly not wanting to part, while rocking her and whispering into her ear, the single phrase that should have released from my mouth long ago, had I known we'd be here today. These words, I should have said the day my hidden truths became secret no more, "I'm so sorry."

Swaying back and forth, feeling the softest most faint release of air dust the side of my neck, with the little energy she had left, one soft and frail tear dropped from Lesley's eye socket to the center of my shirt. Looking down and whipping away the tears from both the pain of her injury and also the pain myself, her husband, and outside forces had caused, with the tiny bit of oxygen remaining in her lungs, Lesley fixed her lips to respond, "I forgive you."

The next thing I knew, Lesley's entire body went limp in my arms and all I had to hold onto were her words. Words of a forgiving soul who had proven once again how amazing she was. To forgive all that I had said and done spoke so much of her character and went to explain why I loved and respected her as I did.

Laying her lifeless body on my lap, my clothing covered entirely in her blood, I placed a kiss onto her forehead, my tears covering her face. Hoping that she would take with her a better image of me than the one that was created under false pretense, I held on to her hand as her soul stood a fine line between heaven and earth.

Dazed and confused at the events that took my precious Lesley from me, I heard not a single announcement by the police as they broke my office door down to get inside and allow the EMT's to administer CPR to my heart which had already left me here to question all that could have been had I stood, man enough to confess not a lie, but the truth about my life as she had done with hers.

Not yet allowing the EMT's access to Lesley's body wanting her with me just a little while longer, I held onto her reflecting on the memorable months she blessed me with, beginning the night I met and fell in love with her.

Attempting to release my arms from her body, "Sir, please let us do our job," I slowly handed her over, broken inside. Following the EMT's from the moment they placed her on the stretcher all the way to the exit of the back door, my hand still attached to Lesley's.

The hurt, hard to contain, watching Lesley placed on a stretcher and wheeled away out of my sight.

The emotion controlling my entire being as she entered into the ambulance, "YOU CAN'T TAKE HER FROM ME."

Held back by the police, attempting to run after Lesley, the officers held me back as best as they could, pleading that I allow personnel to save her, but in my heart, I knew that she was gone. The moment they wheeled her out of the shop, I felt our goodbyes exchanged, knowing that was the final time she would exit out of my life. This realization caused my legs to lose feeling and body to fall to the ground as I watched the EMT's close the ambulance door and remain parked instead of speeding off to the nearest hospital, indicating what I already knew: there was nothing they could do.

My arms extended out, I shouted, "LESLEY," but there was no answer.

After routine questions asked by the police, including whether or not I was her husband due to the amount of emotion displayed, as much as I wanted to turn my nose up at the man who caused so much pain in her life and chose not to appreciate the gem he had in his very eyes that I would kill to hold a little while longer, I realized that he and I were one in the same. If I turned my nose at him, I'd have to look at the mirror and do the same thing to my own reflection. We both took for granted a woman who was crying out to be loved and instead of answering her cries, sat back and filled her heart with lies taking for granted the fact we, or at least myself knew that she would always be here.

With a vague description of the suspect, the police, not much to go one, with my permission, began combing the inside as well as outside perimeter of the building in search of any possible evidence the intruder may have left behind.

Needing to catch my breath, I followed the officers around where I bore witness to numerous bystanders, standing between us a thin line of yellow caution tape. The reporters, pulling into the parking lot alongside one another in competition to air what they considered this to be, a breaking story first.

Little did they know, Lesley was not a story, but a human being who had been through more than enough. So much so, they would have to find another news story to cover because they were not getting any information from me no matter how loud they shouted or pleaded for a few moments of my time as if they truly cared to display any sympathy.

Engine sounding off in the ambulance, in route of the hospital I assumed, I walked forward seeking the well-being of both Lesley and my child. Having not disclosed the pregnancy to anyone else, I would inquire about Lesley first.

From the sound of the truck, I actually felt hopeful that just maybe, she was still here.

The driver of the ambulance, flagging down the nearest officer, awaited Investigator Thompson before both men exchanged words I could not hear, but wanting to know what was going on, I headed in the very direction I could see the EMT hand the officer a chart through the driver side window.

Ignoring the commotion from the curb as the crowd grew, I stood before the officer and fearfully asked one very important question. The ambulance remaining in park, I knew, but wanted to confirm the answer to the question that was burning inside, "How is Lesley?" holding my breath, awaiting the verdict.

Swallowing what appeared to be courage that altered the officer's former behavior, he paused, placed his hand on my shoulder in an attempt to hold back his own emotion, and delivered the news I feared, but knew without a doubt, "I'm sorry sir."

Taking his hand from my shoulder, positioning it onto his head, rubbing his hand on down his face, "She didn't make it."

Turning away from any cameras, not a sole worthy of my emotions as it pertained to the hurtful feeling of life that was lost, I walked away kicking any debris that lay on the ground, placed my hands-on top of my head, and just leaned forward shaking in disbelief.

Finding it hard to accept the fact that she was gone, I just let out my pain as much as anyone else would in time of shock and sorrow.

Removing my hands from my head, I whipped the tears that made a home on my cheekbones and asked if I could have a brief moment with her. Aware that I was not her husband, I was prepared for the officer to tell me no, but viewing the emotion attached to my request, against what I'm sure was protocol when dealing with a crime scene investigation, I was allotted five minutes alone to be near.

Escorting me to the ambulance, the officer with his hat removed from his head as a form of respect for the overall travesty, knocked on the back door of the truck, and asked those inside a moment out so that I could be alone with her just one last time.

Uncertain if I could see her in the condition she was, I

began searching for inner courage to stand above her deceased body.

Tears returning, I contemplated giving up the opportunity to go inside for I could not bear witness to Lesley in the state that she was in knowing I played a role in the smile she had no more.

Thinking hard and searching for words appropriate for a queen and Lesley was my queen whether outsiders believed it or not, I placed my right foot on the first step of the truck, with a heavy breath, used both hands to lift my body inside and as I witnessed her body laying still from a far, I was interrupted and exited the truck, hearing in my left ear, a males voice screaming, "THAT'S MY WIFE. LET ME THROUGH."

Having never been introduced to Lesley's husband or seen any type of visual, I knew that the frantic outcry was Trent, himself. My words would forever remain in my mind and heart as I would now have to make room for this man I'd heard so much about, who had just been made aware of the outcome of the shooting.

"Sir you cannot go in there."

Shouting for Trent to stand back, fearing that he could

potentially contaminate the crime scene, officers held onto to him, who to the human eye appeared devastated learning that Lesley had passed away and if he were anything like myself, had to come to terms knowing there was no longer any time to make his wrongs, right.

It was he who was now front and center of the cameras and although I'm certain no one wanted media exposure, it was Lesley's husband who was the rightful man to be pictured, pleading for the public's help to apprehend the killer, and in no way, shape, or form was he making discrete, his feelings as it pertained to the turmoil the killer caused.

Police alongside of Lesley's husband, walked him in the very direction I stood and for the first time, face to face I met who for so long I deemed my competitor, but today, he was more than I. He was Lesley's husband and I was nothing more than a man of her past who's only qualifications of being in the same place, same time as her husband was that she was shot in my shop where I just so happened to be.

Neither of us stating a single word, only a glare from his eye to mine, the officer broke the ice, extremely thick, and introduced me to Trent, "Sir, this here is Timothy McWilliams. He is the owner of the shop in which your wife was killed."

This being the first day that I had spoken with Lesley in some time, I was not sure what, if anything, Trent knew about myself or his wife for that matter. I said very little and played off of Trent's words alone, wanting not to add anymore hurt than what was already created in the wake of Lesley's untimely death.

Specifically wanting Lesley to hurt no further, I decided it best to leave all that we

shared in a past, a past that had come to an end with no further shot of any future. To Trent, I

was going to be the mechanic who occasionally looked after his wife's car repairs and he, would be my clients husband who I knew nothing more than the name she had once stated.

Extending my hand out of respect and also a means to some form of closure he knew nothing about, I awaited Trent's response once introducing myself, "I'm Timothy."

From all of the pain, a brief intermission of laughter released from my body as Lesley was the only one to call me Timothy whom I had introduced myself as opposed to Tim. It was the little things that brought so much joy to my life. A life that would have to go on forever without her keeping our

Jasmine Herring's, *More Than Enough*
293

memories in my heart, sharing with no one, but my thoughts that would forever reserve a spot for my love.

A blank stare at first, my arm now growing numb, instead of a meeting of the hands, Trent responded with a hug of gratitude instead; a hug in which I was taken back as Lesley had always depicted him as a man without any emotion.

All of us dealing with death differently, I wasn't sure if this was his way of grieving, but nevertheless, there was no sense in me arguing with him, pointing any fingers, or telling him all that I knew he had done. More than anything I was grateful for his actions, as they allowed me to meet a phenomenal woman who made such an impact on my life.

Had he never hurt her to begin, just maybe she and I would not have had the opportunity to cross paths.

Parting, chest from chest as Trent's hug came to a close, he whipped his tears away that had fallen onto the bloodied clothing that still remained pressed against my body. As I turned in the opposite direction, the officers requesting to speak with Trent, I placed my hand on the back of the ambulance truck hoping to take a portion of Lesley's soul with me. Just as I released my hand alongside the vehicle, I heard out in the distance, "Thank you!"

Was this Lesley? Had she come back to life?

Anxiously wanting to know who's voice I could hear, I turned around and stared at the body of the person who extended gratitude. Saddened that it was not Lesley, but Trent.

Why or what was he thanking me for?

Conversing with the officers, I chose not to interrupt. Instead, I nodded back at Trent as he placed his arm halfway up, balled his fist, and extended an act of brotherhood.

Lesley may have been absent from the body, but her way of bringing love and peace was still present here on earth. I truly believe that she had brought both Trent and myself here together to make amends with an act Trent had no idea and I not to reveal. Peace and love, two very important acts she wanted from the world, I was going to do my part and honor in her name. For the love and honor of Lesley, I left my shop holding no grudges and carrying peace in my heart as I hope she had moved enough in Trent for him to do the same.

Hopefully with our exchange, Lesley had entered into

the gates of heaven and was in pain no more.

TRENT

CHAPTER TWENTY-FIVE

MISSING PIECE

It had been nine days, nine days since the murder of my wife and yet not a single lead into her murder had been found. The detectives had the nerve to tell me that they were preparing to close the case as this was the first time in years they had not one single piece of evidence to go on.

With the high traffic in and out of Tim's shop, not one latent finger print lifted could be considered a clue as this was a business many patrons frequented.

After questioning myself, Tim, and a host of coworkers, as I could have told the investigators while they continued wasting time searching dead ends, Lesley had no enemies which is why I truly believed my wife was in the wrong place at the wrong time and lost her life because of it. To think that the man responsible could very well escape the consequences

of his actions was gut wrenching to me. He had no idea the pain that he caused that would leave a permanent hole in my heart. While he walked this earth free, happy, and without remorse to give himself up, I found it hard to go on each day without the love of my life.

They say you don't know what you have until it's gone and the creator of this statement could not have depicted the way I felt more perfectly. For nine days I remained hidden behind the four walls Lesley tried so hard to make a home for she and I with little help from myself as her husband.

From the front door I would walk into and smell the subtle aroma of her Chanel perfume, that would guide me into the kitchen she slaved after work to prepare a hot meal upon my arrival, I missed her. To the living room she would introduce a hot plate knowing I would probably decline, never did she complain or fail to impress me with her devotion and consistent display of love. To the stairs she would walk with her head hanging low as I would selfishly disregard her efforts as a wife, I missed her. To the bedroom she would find herself searching for me as I would leave her lonely to cry herself to sleep, feeling as though her attempts were unwelcomed and without appreciation, I missed my wife.

How desperately I wanted to reverse time and walk into

the house, expressing the same smile on my face that she displayed upon my arrival knowing that she really wanted to frown out of frustration coming home to someone like myself. How desperately I wanted to smell her scent one more time and hold on to it just a little while longer. How desperately I wanted her to sit and relax while I, myself, prepared her a meal as she worked just as hard as I, if not harder dealing with my dysfunctional behaviors. How desperately I wanted to put my personal problems, outside of our marriage, away, long enough for Lesley not to ever have to question or doubt that she was the problem. How desperately I wanted to reverse the time before a single tear dropped from her precious eyes on account of my mistreatment to her. My desperation weighing heavy on me, all I could do now was reminisce on how great she was and how I was never going to gain another opportunity to tell her.

Here I was today, walking down the very aisle we married less than a year ago. Here I was entering into the very building Lesley asked me each and every Sunday to accompany her which I would always turn the other cheek. Both feet planted firmly on the ground, I was finally here, this time to view my wife's still and lifeless body resting inside of a casket which you could have never prepared me for.

Led to my seat, along with my mother, coworker Traci,

and his wife, I could see the choir rise to sing and with the ushers closing the doors of the church, my wife's homegoing service had officially begun.

A stranger to the church for some time now, I could not understand why everyone was nodding their heads to the music sounding from the pulpit. Numerous guests standing while holding an angelic expression on their faces and I did not know whether or not to take offense or simply let it be. Were they unaware that we were here to mourn a life taken away and not a social gathering? Was I the only one left here on earth to grieve the loss of my wife?

If the pain in my heart wasn't enough to bear, the somber keystrokes the pianist played as the song For Every Mountain began to play, sure took a toll. Allowing my mother to make the musical selections for the service, I was not expecting to hear songs destined to draw out even more sadness that clearly, I was the only one in which the effects were triggered.

Had it not been for my mother who loved Lesley like the daughter she never had and my right-hand man Traci, now my new business partner who I planned to introduce to Lesley that day, I would have just walked out the moment the funeral director lowered the top of Lesley's casket.

This here and this day was a terrible dream I so desperately wanted to wake from for I would never wish these agonizing days on my worst enemy.

Rubbing my eyes with the knuckles of my thumbs, I tried to hold back the painful tears we as men often try hard to hide to save face. Finding it hard to do, I lowered my head inside the obituary I had to gain the strength to create, retelling Lesley's beginning and short ending which was lost with no prior knowledge.

Little did she know, I loved the hair color she had recently applied to each strand; so much so, I snuck and took a picture as she assumed that I was avoiding her presence and spending too much time on my phone. A picture I would stare at daily when the words would not flow as we ignored each other's paths. Having no idea that I would be using this image as her final bow for the world to see, the wounds hurt a little more as yet again, I was not man enough to express my desire for her beauty or even reference the change to her outer features.

The first song coming to a close, I could see the pastor in deep thought holding on to his bible as he would soon deliver the eulogy that would send my wife off to paradise.

It would be a lie if I said that I was not mad at God for allowing my wife to die. If anyone deserved a tragic end, it certainly was not Lesley. Why didn't he just take me? From the number of individuals from all walks of life, some knowing my wife only from the telling of the news, it was clear that she was very impactful to many and for God to allow her to die so brutally, I was having a hard time understanding.

My mother, rubbing my back as the tears began to resurface, this time the tears a result of pure anger. I continued looking around in the crowd and still, everyone was smiling and swaying their heads and arms to the melody in which the choir sung as if they were in the center of the dance floor. The only saving grace for those I wanted to approach and dismiss from my wife's funeral on account of their behavior which I found most inappropriate, was the constant snapshot of the day which my life fell apart.

What if I never left out of the house that day? Lesley would not have gone to the shop. Why did she feel the urgency to have her car looked at? I told her that I would take care of it. What if I were there just before she passed? Just maybe, my words would have healed her enough to stay with me. So many promises I would have made and stood by just to have her here today. Would she have had the strength to hold on if she knew how grateful I was for her love even though I pushed it away time and time again?

Resting my head on my mother's shoulder as she attempted to console me, I witnessed the entire room stand as the choir took the song up a few octaves, spirits now raised. The entire room on their feet, I could see the tears began to pour, mine never ending, and finally, I could see others in agreeance of my sorrow. The smiles remaining on some, however; I was no longer going to assume what anyone else was feeling or thinking, but myself.

The words to the song, "Why do you cry? He has risen. Why are you weeping? He's not dead." Hearing these words, I could feel my anger transition into peace. I could actually sense my wife near, standing next to God, assuring me that she was ok and well. This feeling I was made to feel aided my understanding of the behavior the room had to begin with that I first, was confused by.

Many lifelong members of the church, fully aware that going to heaven although sad to loved ones, was a reward we were all trying to win. For standing alongside of the Lord was the ultimate prize of a job well done here on earth and my Lesley certainly gave many reason to salute her.

I too, began to stand. Having not once been led by a song before in my entire life, I no longer looked at my wife's funeral as a place to mourn tragedy, but instead, one to rejoice and celebrate the life of my queen which I believed many were already participating, myself taking a little while longer. It was at this very moment where I can confess, I finally felt the spirit of the Lord move inside of me for the first time. This was a place I believe my wife was attempting to get me to for such a long period of time and feeling as though her presence were near, I hoped that she was able to capture this moment.

Everyone still standing, many in deep thought and prayer meditation, it was one voice, separated by any other, that stood out from the crowd. The voice, a bit louder than most, slightly stronger in feeling, displayed a deeper, darker emotion than any other in the room.

Normal for members to continue praising well after the choir ended their final notes, a reason many Christian churches exceed standard service time, the pastor remained silent at the pulpit, respecting and welcoming the praises displayed.

The pianist continuing to play to the tune of the unfamiliar face who began walking down the aisle while all others had since returned to their seats.

Assuming she was walking in the direction of a nearby pew, the music began to fade cueing for the pastor to take his stand, "Amen." Signaling that the message was gearing up, the pastor looked out to the crowd and allowed God to use him through spoken word.

Known for making light of a trial often hard to bear, the pastor opened with a bit of comedy in attempts to soothe the hurt. Now I'd been told that his jokes were far from funny, but the accent he spoke to go along with his humor or shall I say, lack thereof, made the day a little lighter and a bit comical, "That choir can sang yall. I mean they can really sang."

Gaining the attention of the members who saw fit to celebrate with us, the pastor asked everyone to bow their heads in a moment of prayer, "Let's bow our heads."

Having yet to deliver a full sentence, the pastor was interrupted by the same mysterious woman who had yet to take her seat. Although the piano was no longer making a sound, this did not stop the woman from making her own music, her voice loud, visible to the audience.

You could see the agitation of the pastor, but wanting not to be rude, understanding we all deal with death differently, he responded instead, "Amen sister."

I had never seen this woman before, but as she made her way to the front of the sanctuary and rested on Lesley's casket, I felt compelled to rise from my seat and console her as I would assume she was close with Lesley with the overwhelming emotion she made public. Excusing myself from my mother, Traci, and even giving a head nod to the pastor to postpone for a brief moment, I stood near this broken woman whose head lay face down on the top of Lesley's casket, screaming that it be opened so that she could see her. Unsure of what to say or do, I placed my hand gently on her back and did the one thing I knew Lesley would have done. I leaned forward and released from my mouth a prayer of deliverance and peace. I prayed that God would free from this woman the pain that consumed her. That she would be shown like myself and many others, that Lesley was resting well with our Lord, Jesus Christ.

Raising her head up, turning her body in front of me, I backed up, our eyes now meeting for the first time.

With complete silence in the building, many onlookers in sight, I remained still and watched as the woman reached her palm towards the back of my head. Drawing me near, she moved close, positioning her lips towards my left ear for all to see. With a cracked voice she asked, "Are you Trent?"

As I had been on the news pleading for my wife's murderer to come forward, I'm sure she was able to determine who I was by either witnessing myself on television or others in the sanctuary who may have pointed me out. My response, still curious of this woman's identity, I cautiously answered, "I am."

She looked at me holding her lips together, shed one single tear, held out a white envelope and asked I wait to open until the conclusion of the service. Her hands inside of mine, she concluded our rather awkward introduction with, "I'm so sorry."

As many had already extended their sympathy, it was something about this woman's grievance that was a bit different. It lingered and made me question the contents inside of the envelope that I had just received.

Curious, along with everyone else whose eyes had remained glued to the front of the church, I went back to my seat and signaled for the pastor to continue, hoping to get us all back to the reason we were here to begin.

My mother, just as curious as to the meaning of the

public display brought on by this woman, leaned over to my side inquiring, "What was that about Trent?" with a look as if I had some explaining to do.

Making it very clear, as to the eye it may have seemed as if this unfamiliar stranger was my hidden lover due to her impromptu mannerisms, I'd never seen her before today. I may have done a lot of wrong in my marriage, but never had I even thought to cheat on my wife if that is what my mother or anyone else depicted in their minds.

Responding just as lost myself, with a shrug of my shoulders, I whispered back, "I've never seen her before Mom."

Holding on to the letter of great mystery, my mother proceeded to ask a follow up question, not sure whether or not she received my first response. When I say she loved Lesley, I mean she loved Lesley and would protect her until the end even before myself, her very own son, "Then what is the letter in your hand from this so called strange woman?"

From the short interaction with this woman, I began to feel pressured and in need of an alibi as my mother did not appear convinced that I knew nothing of this woman.

Those present near and far, eyes remaining in my

direction, the pastor even a bit confused, possibly changing from a delivery of a eulogy to that of infidelity in the church house.

Fidgety to say the least, not patient enough to wait for the close of service as instructed by the woman who had everyone forming opinions in their heads about my loyalty, I unfolded the envelope as the seal had been tucked in, not licked. To myself, I quietly began reading word after word to make sense of this not so normal introduction while attempting to keep one eye on the pastor who proceeded with the eulogy in spite of the temporary intermission brought on.

Squeezing the letter together with both hands, the pressure too intense for the fibers, out from my palm it fell to the ground. With great speed and without warning, I exited the building through the center aisle in search of the author of this letter whose words, painted a clear picture of her urgency to speak with me and to some, her momentary insanity.

Plowing through the double doors that took me out into the foyer, I whisked through the exit and into the parking lot faster than lightning. Left, right, front and back I searched, but could not find this woman who had revealed a hidden truth I thought I may never receive on my journey to find closure.

My mother, along with other members who once occupied seats in the sanctuary all rushed out to view as I ran from car to car, searching for a needle in a haystack.

Screaming from a far, I could hear my mother shout out, "TRENT," with a voice of confusion and worry having to answer by herself, why her son was running around like a crazy man, but this moment was far too great to respond or end my desperate search.

Up and down I continued through the parking lot and my mission, so focused that nothing or no one person could make me lose sight until, "POP." A loud, almost firecracker sound rattled into one ear and out of the other with a lingering ring, pausing my efforts for a brief moment and causing a few to scream as they too, were startled.

Glancing around, but seeing nothing out of the ordinary, I assumed what sounded like a firecracker, was either a busted tire, a finder bender amongst two cars, or construction.

Having searched each and every row of the parking lot making certain that no one exited, I came across one final row and out from a distance, I could see a body, still in the driver seat of a navy-blue dodge neon.

Calling out, "Ma'am," but there was no response or movement. I proceeded forward, but treaded lightly with much caution as I was now one with the driver side door.

Knocking on the window, still receiving no response, I attempted to jiggle the handle of the front door, but to no avail would it open. Calling out one final time, I headed towards the front of the car where I noticed her head and eyes facing, hoping that whatever was distracting her, she could remove herself and make sense of a letter that I would not bring myself to believe.

Head down in disbelief, hands planted on the hood of the car keeping hold of the balance I thought I may lose, reality struck and I learned all remaining answers to the questions I sought, would forever be a mystery, one in which I could only guess and further assume.

She was the missing piece to the puzzle not yet put together. She was the answer to so many questions I had inside. Now she was gone due to a self-inflicted wound to the head. A bloody mass that seeped down to her face, dripping past her still lips that from the letter, had been crying out for some time.

The crowd becoming impatient, it was a matter of

moments before many saw that I had ceased further movement and joined right behind me to view the very image I was still in awe of.

Asking everyone, all souls desperate to get a glimpse of what was now a suicide scene the police were in route of, I pleaded that everyone step back as I opened the only entrance accessible, the passenger side door where I was introduced to yet a second letter that on top, lay what I believed to be a pregnancy test. Removing both items from the seat, I sat them on the roof of the car. Needing to occupy the front seat, in attempts to check for a pulse which to touch was extremely faint and almost non-existent.

Sitting next to the woman who had since, slouched over, onlooker praying, some screaming, "JESUS." I began to pray myself as my wife remained dead inside of the church we all exited, myself, the only party to know who this woman truly was.

I prayed, that like my wife, I hoped that this woman who had much pain that she had been battling for some time now, was free from all that had consumed her for many years.

With my eyes closed, hand on hers, squeezing it in

preparation of closing out the prayer with an, "Amen," I felt the slightest most frail squeeze back. Mumbling what may have been her final words, I lifted closer from my seat and placed my ear almost to her lips where she asked, "Wasn't I more than enough?"

And just like that, her hand released its tiny amount of pressure it had supplied to mine, and with us, she was no longer.

The sirens closer and closer, I was reintroduced to the same detectives who were in process of closing my wife's case. With the information I now had in my possession, no longer was I holding them accountable for finding answers, for they now rested in my hand. One letter followed by the next, I turned them over to the officers and just like that, the case was solved.

Yellow caution tape now aligned the perimeter of the car, all bystanders asked to move as paramedics removed the missing link from the car. Placed on a stretcher, she was slowly wheeled away, a white sheet covering her identity.

Finally having all of the answers I needed, still I found myself unsatisfied and without the closure I thought I would gain knowing the truth. Instead, I was more hurt than before falling to my knees, shouting to God, "WHY?"

Jasmine Herring's, *More Than Enough*

To another, the events closing this day out would prove therapeutic, but for me, I was left further confused. On one hand, I felt God granting me peace and on the other, the Devil intervening and leaving me in further dysfunction. My heart cried out for not myself, but for another man. A man whom the second letter was addressed to that the police now had in their chain of custody. A man, whom I looked in the eye the day that my wife died who I now knew was the true and final link to the closure I was in desperate need of.

CHAPTER TWENTY-SIX

WITHOUT YOU

"You can do this man," supporting words from my new-found friend who knew much about me, myself only recently learning of him. Our bond, that much stronger as we stood alongside one another, grieving similar pain, stemmed by very similar circumstances.

Could I do this? I began to doubt, but had to at least try for the sake of my bleeding hearts ultimate healing. A heart I wanted to share with the one person who cared, no longer here in the physical presence.

A man of few words, I left behind who I was yesterday, decided to take a stand as a man and come clean, releasing the soul I selfishly contained inside, but would she hear me? That became a mystery.

With every step I took up the hill, I could feel a force pulling me back and a voice in my ear taunting me to turn around. The old me, quiet and reserved, would have listened, but the new Trent, forever changed, had to press on and continue walking forward.

Separating from one another's side, I allowed my dear friend the time that he needed, him returning the same act on my behalf while I took in the scenery that surrounded such a beautiful landmark; Lesley's headstone.

It's funny how relationships are often formed especially when it is without intent and here we gathered today. Acquaintances for a short period of time, one could conclude that there was no chance of our strengthened bond going anywhere any time soon. As crazy as our history was, he was the only one that understood me now that Lesley was gone and could also relate, molding our friendship into a brotherhood, "I'll be right here if you need me man," shouted from one plot to another.

I lowered my body to the ground where I sat on a bed of freshly cut grass which furnished the very tomb I rested my head. Maybe if I placed my ear close enough to the outer layer, just maybe I would hear her soft voice or feel just one tiny heartbeat.

My knees high to my chest, arms holding them closed, I rested my head right at my kneecaps as I pondered on what I would say first.

"Man, I miss you," the first four words to muffle from my mouth which remained pressed against my legs.

Getting a bit emotional, I chose to stand before my wife as a sign of respect. Sadness mixed with anger, I began to kick the pebbles which were sprinkled underneath the concrete my feet rested upon. Feeling as though I were to blame for the direction our marriage shifted and ended, all I could do was fall to my knees, squeezing my face together in hopes of keeping the tears from hindering my words, "I'm sorry Baby. I'm so very sorry."

With only myself to blame, I rose from the ground, stepped back, and stood on the concrete path which I used as a platform.

Looking up to the sky and back down at Lesley's headstone, unsure of where my eyes should focus, I noticed a beautiful ray of sunlight next to Lesley's name, reflecting near my chest.

Glancing back up at the sky, I began to smile as I felt this

Lesley's sense of humor raining down on me, sending a sign that she was very much with me, listening, wanting me to know that she forgave me.

Removing the tears that flowed in between my fingers as I attempted to catch them with the palms of my hands, I began to chuckle as I continued speaking as if Lesley were actually standing beside me, "You probably won't believe me, but this past month, I've had so much time to reflect all alone and Lesley, I want you to know, life just isn't the same without you."

Thinking of all that I took for granted and would never get back, made me miss her so much more.

"I come home to a lonely house that was once showered with love. I enter the kitchen in hopes of smelling the scent of your cooking and I find nothing. I sit on the couch, the one that aligns directly in plain eye sight of the front door, just waiting for your smiling face to walk through. Waking up the next morning on the very couch I waited, realizing, you're never coming home again and the smile I yearn for, just to see once more, is gone forever."

Shaking my head, ashamed, reminiscing on my many

faults, I asked aloud, "How did you put up with me all this time? How did you find the strength to even smile?"

Looking over my shoulder, checking on my friend who was clearly in deep conversation and seeing that he was not prepared to leave, I used this time as an opportunity to explain myself further.

"Do you remember the day I asked if I could go to church with you?"

Taking in the sway of the trees throughout the cemetery, the squirrels running and skipping between the tombstones, and the sun beaming down on me, I awaited a response to my question, knowing that it would not be one of a verbal act, but maybe a slight difference in nature.

Holding off a few more seconds, I continued on.

"I could tell on your face that you were taken back by my out of the blue accompaniment. I knew that you were in disbelief and assumed that I was all talk and not seriously committing to entering into a house you continuously walked in, alone, hoping to find me by your side."

Filling my inner cheeks with air, one side at a time, I

moved forward.

"With a one-track mind to get things in order in my home, I thought going to church was most appropriate and a great first step to win your heart back. The second you drove off, I rushed upstairs to find something appropriate to wear and in the midst of leaping into the closet, I must have tripped over a box in the corner of your side. Looking down and noticing the lid no longer attached to the box, I noticed your beautiful face, slightly hidden underneath your wedding veil. Curious as to what else the box contained, I grabbed hold of the bottom and rested on our bedroom mattress where I began replaying our wedding day one photo at a time. The day we both said, "I Do."

Choking back any further words, I paused to regroup and process the upcoming syllables that were preparing to leak from my mouth next.

Listening to the solid footsteps drawing near, I watched as my friend ended his personal conversation and stood back, allowing me to finish my very own before exiting the cemetery.

Standing approximately ten feet behind me, he placed his hands behind his back, lowered his head, and waited.

Turning back around to face my queen, I swallowed my pride, "If I were in your shoes, having to deal with someone like myself, having to cry yourself to sleep at the frustration of constant rejection, feeling unappreciated, not being treated as you truly deserved to be, Lesley, I probably would have done the same thing. I placed you right into his arms and that is an act I cannot take back let alone stomach."

Embarrassed at myself, I looked behind me, motioned with a wave of my hand for my friend to stand beside me for I wanted to be a man of openness, not secrets. "You needed me and time and time again, I turned my back. You begged for my love and I made you feel that you were the problem. I can only imagine how that made you feel inside. I broke you down and I'm finding it so hard to live with that burden."

Leaning forward as these words were hard to say, I was consoled by my friend who delivered a pat to the back as a sign that he was here for support.

One breath after another, feeling poorly about the result of my actions, I explained, "Lesley. Baby. My rock. I never had an example that taught me how to truly love a person, myself included. Of course, my mother was always there for me and adored you, but growing up, she was so focused on finding a man, at times she forgot that she was also raising one. I never learned how to take care of a heart. I never learned how to be sensitive and compassionate to your feelings. So used to you giving all of the love, I became accustomed to only receiving. I heard your cries, but knew you'd always be around and that once I got it together, you would accept me with open arms and welcome me into your heart like you'd done time and time again."

Placing my hands on top of my head, "The night you said that you would either leave or cheat, I took those words as threats with no promise to ever act or commit. I found you incapable of going anywhere on account that you had never gone nowhere before."

Taking a few steps forward and bowing down, knees embedded in the ground, I held on to Lesley's grave, wrapping my arms tightly around and placed a burning assumption to rest.

"I may have said and done a lot of things to break your heart, but Baby, as God is my witness, never ever did I cheat on you. That betrayal," lifting my cheeks to turn my head left and right, in disbelief that I would even be labeled a cheater, "not me at all."

Jasmine Herring's, *More Than Enough*

"When you asked me about Traci, he was a coworker battling like myself to keep our jobs. What I didn't tell you because I did not want you to worry, was that both Traci, myself, along with a few others were up for termination as the company planned to downsize and eliminate those making the most. Lesley, as a man, I could not tell you that my job was in jeopardy. I could not tell you that you may be responsible for our bills for an extended period of time. I could not tell you that the life you were accustomed to may be shifting. My actions, although unacceptable, were out of fear, having nothing to do with you as a wife. Baby you were perfect."

Wishing I could have said all of this earlier, "Had I known this day may have been avoided had I been upfront to begin with, I would have told you this, the moment it started weighing on my conscience and tearing me up inside."

Counting on my hand, the heinous acts one by one, "The strip club over your birthday, the sudden urge to go out of town, the constant attacking and bickering, all me, not you."

"At the time, our bosses wanted us to party with them. As much as I'd rather have been home with you watching that silly Lifetime channel, I had to prove myself worthy, even if it meant going against my morals and disregarding your birthday

Jasmine Herring's, *More Than Enough*

324

which I felt terrible the moment I stepped foot out of the house. When I went away for a while, it was not to meet another female, but to seek out new clients to further grow the business and prove why the company needed to keep me. But the worst of all and this has me mortified, when you looked me in the eye with an ultimatum, at first tickled about, had I known I pushed you that far, I would have said, 'Fuck my job,' just to have my wife."

Reaching back, asking my friend for the envelope, both familiar with the contents held inside, Lesley unaware, "The day the officers knocked on our door and told me of your injuries, at first confused, as I had just walked in the door assuming that you remained at the dinner table. Assuming they had the wrong house, I curiously searched the dining room table to find you were in fact, gone. Thoughts running a mile a second, I allowed the fellow officers to drive me to the location you were supposedly shot. A building I had been made aware prior due to the very descriptive imagery detailed in your diary which happened to also rest in the box containing our wedding photos.

Uncertain as to the severity of your injuries, I was in a state of shock that anyone could or would want to place harm on you. Pondering on all of the changes I was prepared and already making, I could not wait to get to you and nurse you back to health quick and fast.

Pulling up and released from the front seat of the escorting officers patrol car, I plunged my feet on the stomping ground that had become a therapeutic and reoccurring stop for you and although I had no right and deserved the feelings inside, an overwhelming amount of jealousy surrounded my entire being.

Seeing the numerous news anchors, reporting live, all with the most serious and unchanging facial structures, what at first I assumed a minor injury you had sustained on account of what the officers had yet to inform me, I knew time was not on my side.

With a one-track mind to find you, I began scouring through the high traffic just past the yellow caution tape. Hoping to either see you on a stretcher or laying down receiving medical attention, I angled at the ambulance in the back corner that remained idle, but with lights flashing.

One foot off the ground, preparing to jog over to you, in the corner of my ear I heard a report say, "BREAKING NEWS. Police have confirmed that the female shooting victim, whose name will not be released until family members have been notified, has died."

It was if someone had those words on repeat as they continued to play in my ear, "BREAKING NEWS. POLICE HAVE CONFIRMED THAT THE FEMALE SHOOTING VICTIM, WHOSE NAME WILL NOT BE RELEASED UNTIL FAMILY MEMBERS HAVE BEEN NOTIFIED, HAS DIED."

In a state of shock, disheartenment, confusion, and quite unaware of what happened from the time I stepped out of the house to now, all feelings wrapped into one, I just shouted, "Lesley," praying that you would answer me and that this would all amount to a case of mistaken identity. That another man would take my place, having to grieve the loss of his wife and not myself.

Punching the air until the officers were drawn at the behaviors I displayed, I was assisted and led to the ambulance where I was introduced to at first, a person I thought a paramedic. Covered from head to toe in your blood, I gathered he and other personnel had attempted to resuscitate your lifeless body with failed attempts as he stepped down from and exited the back door of the ambulance.

The introduction, not as I expected by officers, I learned that he in fact was not a paramedic, but ironically a person who had aided you in the past, each and every time I caused pain. He was the man who you, yourself credited for reviving you from a lifeless relationship. What hurt the most, he was the one there to hold your hand until you released your final breath.

Jealous and angry at first, I humbled myself and began to process all that I had learned and now seen from more than just today.

Standing toe to toe, I looked at him differently than most would in my situation. I did not see a man who had been intimate with my wife. I did not point the blame at him for tearing up my marriage. I did not see a man who would soon become the father to my wife's unborn, making me a step parent.

What I saw instead was a mirror image of all that my wife needed, begged for, and received. I could not be those things for a long period of time, but looking at this man who could be, all I had left in me to say to him, "Thank you!"

Lesley deserved the world and while mine was crashing before my eyes, I was not focused on the fact that throughout my battles, the toughest battle was in my home. The war was being fought between my wife and I. She wanted love and I refused to return all that she showed. She wanted a family and I declined that dream. She wanted to smile and I gave her reason to cry. She wanted public displays of affection and I hid it all behind closed doors. She wanted communication and I gave her secrecy. She needed a man and I gave her someone else's hand.

No matter what Tim may or may not have known, he wasn't to blame. He may have been the other man, but for the last few months of Lesley's life, he was THE MAN. Where I lacked, he picked up my slack. My wife was whole again. I only wished I could have credited myself for such an act.

It's taken me a while to forgive the person responsible for your death. They took away my second chance to start over and soothe your heart and wounds caused by my lack thereof. For a while I even hated them. I hated them so much that I wished the very pain if not more.

This took some time, but I had to ask myself, "What would Lesley do?"

You had no hate in your heart even for me; pain of

course, but not hate. How could I hate a person that you loved and loved you back?

I hated her until I learned of her internal soul. Learning of her story, my hate turned into sympathy. I only wish that we could have all helped her before it went too far, and the pain no longer able to stand.

She wanted me to tell you how sorry she was Lesley. She wanted you to know that you were not the one to blame. She wanted me to tell you that she looked up to and loved you like the sister she never had. She only wished you would have come to her. So full of life, she knew nothing of your pain. Had she known only an ounce of what you, yourself were dealing with, not only would she have been able to help you, but she may have forgotten some of her very own problems. Helping someone else may have been therapeutic for her as it had worked in your favor.

With only one thing left to say, I unfolded the envelope that became damp from the sweat in my hand, took a few steps forward and read the contents, "I now know why you went to Tim's shop that day. I know how much this pregnancy was eating away at you. I know that you were unsure of how to approach me, whether or not I would stay or go, which I would have remained right by your side, but what you didn't know, which was a total shock to me as well on account of my absence, the tests confirmed, Tim was NOT the father of the baby you were carrying, I WAS."

The family you always wanted, despite my ways, God granted us. I'm sorry you'll never get to experience motherhood and that I will never get to meet my son or daughter, but Baby I want you to know that you would have been an amazing mother and I would have welcomed our child with open arms. I wanted to be a better man for the both of you. I'll never forget you my love or our child.

Closing the test results from the lab and placing them back inside of the envelope, I planted a kiss to my wife's grave and headed towards the car with my friend, who out of respect, had furthered himself and bowed his head down slightly to tears.

"Hey Tim! You ready man?"

Delivering a brother to brother hug as we both had a few blows over the last few weeks bringing us here today. We each took a gasp of air, made our peace with our loved ones and walked towards the new direction God had for our lives.

THE

BIGGEST

FAN

Jasmine Herring's, *More Than Enough*
332

CHAPTER TWENTY-SEVEN

REVELATIONS

Dear Lesley,

I watched the news tonight and learned that it was you. It was you that I shot and killed and I beg to express my apologies. I cannot begin to tell the world how sorry I am for allowing my personal pain to take our dear loved one away. You were so much to so many people including myself. You were my sister, my friend, and the one I wanted to appoint, my child's God Mother. That's right, I wasn't ready to tell anyone, but I was finally pregnant, finally out of the danger zone and feeling fine and well. Listening to all of your coaching, I decided to go and deliver the news to my husband who was uninformed, hoping that this pregnancy would get our marriage back on track and rekindle the love that used to burn, full of desire and passion. Surprising him at his office as I had never done before out of respect for his place of work, I was extremely excited and nervous to tell him that finally, we were going to start a family of our own after battling infidelity and two miscarriages.

Assuming that he was busy with the door cracked, I waited outside until either he stepped out or the female voice ceased in conversation. So ready to start our family, I was devastated and crushed to hear the woman confess that yet again, my husband had fathered her child.

Enraged past the point of no return, I simply couldn't take it anymore. My mind and actions were no longer my own and when I shot you, I only saw the back of your head. I only saw the woman who had taken my opportunity to place a smile on my husband's face. A woman who was filling another void in my husband's life. I don't even remember saying anything or watching your body fall to the ground. I only remember pulling the trigger and witnessing the smile on husband's face turn to the same pain that he had graced me with for all this time.

I wanted to finally take something away from him as he continued taking from me. I needed you, but you never answered. I needed you to tell me that everything would work out as you had told me time and time again.

Thinking that I would be fine having injured the woman who

would be bringing another child into the world with my husband, I could not stomach knowing that it was you.

Seeing you in the casket and witnessing a room filled with loved ones mourning your death because of me, I could not live with my actions. I could not raise a child in a world where their mother would forever be depressed hanging on to a dark secret. A world where the father was forever distraught as he had confessed in the past to loving and wanting to be with a woman I later learned was you.

What I hate him most for is making me feel that all these women had taken something from me when in fact, he was to blame for every tear shed including yours. I guess I was never good enough and that my love wasn't deep enough for him to fight the urge to cheat and betray our marriage.

Lesley, I now know that you were unaware that he was married and for that, I am further sorry for your pain and the pain that I caused. I can no longer go on in life with this burden. If we do not meet again in heaven as I am not sure God will welcome me after what I've done to you, please know, I love you!

Your biggest fan,
Stacy Marie McWilliams
(wife of Timothy McWilliams)

I look at each of you now

And notice that there is not a single face

that doesn't appear down

I do not want you to cry for me,

but instead, listen closely

Don't yearn for too much,

because what you often have

is more than enough

About the Author

Jasmine 'Lanae' Herring was born and raised in Indianapolis, Indiana. A wife and mother of three, the new author is on the rise to becoming one of the best, well-written female authors.

A social butterfly, Jasmine utilizes her interpersonal skills to shape and develop suspenseful dramas that readers are sure to relate. It is simply impossible to open a Jasmine Herring story and not find yourself on a journey in which you have either traveled in the past or are currently trailing.

When asked what's next for the rising author, her response simply put, "Endless stories to cure hearts."

Black Butterfly Books

an imprint of
The Butterfly Typeface Publishing.
Books to intelligently entertain the discriminating reader!
Contact us for all your
publishing & writing needs!

Iris M Williams
PO Box 56193
Little Rock AR 72215

www.butterflytypeface.com